What people are saying about ...

THE FACE OF THE DEEP

"Out of the recent desert of writings on the empowering presence of God comes this book. Creative, thoughtful, rooted, mysterious—it pairs well for a conversation about God's activity in the world."

John Mark Comer, author of *The Ruthless Elimination of Hurry* and pastor of vision and teaching at Bridgetown Church

"*The Face of the Deep* is grounded in Scripture and steeped in awe and wonder. This exploration of the Person and work of the Holy Spirit is creative, thorough, and profound—and as much-needed as it is refreshing."

Karen Swallow Prior, PhD, author of *On Reading Well*

"Paul J. Pastor has given us an icon in prose. Words spark from the pages to display with brilliant color the vitality and beauty of the Spirit. Not content to let the Holy Spirit be merely a theological confession or an experiential aberration, Pastor calls us beyond the face of the deep to experience the mystery of life with the Spirit."

Glenn Packiam, associate senior pastor of New Life Church and author of *Blessed Broken Given* and *Worship and the World to Come*

"Often while reading *The Face of the Deep*, I had to pause, think, and reread a passage too rich and too insightful for a single consideration. Moreover, what hooked me first to that passage were its sharp images and its stout language. I have no doubt that anyone who does not skim but attends closely to Pastor's book will experience the same inspiring jolts."

Walter Wangerin Jr., winner of the National
Book Award for *The Book of the Dun Cow*

"A theologically rich, soul-stirring vision of what the life of the Spirit looks like. This book is a great step forward in helping us have ministries that not only preach the gospel but do so with power, deep conviction, and the Holy Spirit."

Jon Tyson, lead pastor of Church of the
City and author of *Beautiful Resistance*

"This portrait of the presence, power, and work of the Holy Spirit pulsates with awe, wonder, and worship befitting the topic. It's an insightful theological work that feels more like devotional poetry! Full of organic imagery, lively metaphor, and lyrical description, *The Face of the Deep* is a great read. I recommend this for anyone desiring a deeper awareness of the mysterious and beautiful Spirit."

Brett McCracken, senior editor at The Gospel
Coalition and author of *Uncomfortable*

"Paul is perhaps the perfect guide on this journey of mystery—he has been both wounded and healed as he has discovered the Spirit at work all around us. For those like myself who have a hard time articulating with words how the Great Fire has burned us to the core, this book comes as close to it as any I have ever read."

D. L. Mayfield, author of *Assimilate or Go Home* and *The Myth of the American Dream*

"My friend Paul J. Pastor is *himself* a stunning mural unto the creativity and grace of the Creator God. *The Face of the Deep* is a beautiful and brilliant book that will restore the church's heart to the Creator Spirit for ages to come."

Dr. A. J. Swoboda, associate professor of Bible, Theology, and World Christianity at Bushnell University and author of *After Doubt*

"Too often we reduce the Holy Spirit to a stale doctrine or a mechanical force, and that's assuming we acknowledge him at all. What Paul J. Pastor has done with this book is remarkable. He not only opens our eyes to the many facets of the Spirit we have overlooked, but he does it with a beauty that is evidence of the Spirit's presence. He is a craftsman of words and a gift to the church in its contemporary wilderness."

Skye Jethani, author of *With* and the *With God Daily* devotional at WithGodDaily.com

"At last here's a book where the elegance of the prose befits its strange and beautiful subject. *The Face of the Deep* is a collection of personal essays that masterfully mine theology, history, nature, and art for fresh insights into the Spirit's character and work in the world. This book will leave readers enlightened and strangely warmed. Radiant."

Drew Dyck, editor, author of *Yawning at Tigers* and *Your Future Self Will Thank You*

"This breathtaking work is poetic, rich, and deep with the things of God, inviting us to see the world afresh through new eyes. This is a book I didn't know I needed about the God I expect many of us will be surprised to discover has been there all along."

Joshua Ryan Butler, lead pastor of Redemption Tempe and author of *The Skeletons in God's Closet* and *The Pursuing God*

"With imagination and prose, Paul J. Pastor helps us discover the limits of ourselves quickly and profoundly, so we may move with him to discover deep and accessible mystery in God. *The Face of the Deep* opens us to the certainty of uncertainty, which is sure to change mundane binaries and trivial conversations about the Spirit, directing us to new conversations full of life and beauty."

Randy S. Woodley, distinguished professor of faith and culture at George Fox University/ Portland Seminary and author of *Decolonizing Evangelicalism, The Harmony Tree, Shalom and the Community of Creation,* and *Living in Color*

"Having tuned his eyes and ears to the presence of the Holy Spirit in everyday life, Paul J. Pastor's vivid writing breathes life into the mysterious third person of the Trinity. Few books make knowing God more energizing and more enticing than *The Face of the Deep*."

C. Christopher Smith, founding editor of *The Englewood Review of Books* and author of *Slow Church* and *How the Body of Christ Talks*

"What happens when a mathematician writes sonnets? I don't know ... but I now know what it looks like for a poet to write theology. So much of theology is sterile precision ... like an arithmetic table. Such analysis has purpose to be sure, but is of little nourishment to a soul such as mine. This is a book I needed, both in subject and in spirit. *The Face of the Deep* is a surprising spiritual gift."

Tony Kriz, author of *Aloof*

"In *The Face of the Deep*, Paul J. Pastor brings lively wisdom to bear on the often-neglected subject of the Holy Spirit. Artfully and keenly written, these explorations penetrate the surface and bring theological clarity without attempting to extinguish the mystery. A spiritual breath of fresh air."

Paul Louis Metzger, PhD, professor of Christian theology and theology of culture at Multnomah Biblical Seminary and author of *Connecting Christ*

The FACE *of the* DEEP

The *FACE* of the *DEEP*

Experiencing the Beautiful Mystery
of Life with the Spirit

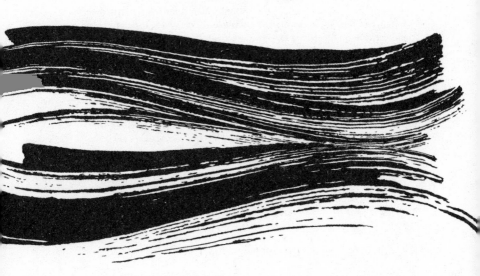

PAUL J. PASTOR

DAVID C COOK

transforming lives together

THE FACE OF THE DEEP
Published by David C Cook
4050 Lee Vance Drive
Colorado Springs, CO 80918 U.S.A.

Integrity Music Limited, a Division of David C Cook
Brighton, East Sussex BN1 2RE, England

The graphic circle C logo is a registered trademark of David C Cook.

The website addresses recommended throughout this book are offered as a
resource to you. These websites are not intended in any way to be or imply an
endorsement on the part of David C Cook, nor do we vouch for their content.

LCCN 2015949963
ISBN 978-0-8307-8133-1
eISBN 978-0-8307-8134-8

The Team: Andrew Stoddard, Tim Peterson, Andy Meisenheimer, Nick
Lee, Laura Weller, Helen Macdonald, Judy Gillispie, Susan Murdock
Cover Design: Nick Lee
Cover Illustrations: Nick Lee and Getty Images
Interior Illustrations: Martin French

Printed in the United States of America
Second Edition 2020

1 2 3 4 5 6 7 8 9 10

060920

CONTENTS

FOREWORD

One of the most important human activities is seeking to know God. As Christians, we pray, gather together, read Scripture, develop cohesive doctrines of who God is and how he works. But I fear that, for some of us, our theology has become more science than art, more theory than experience.

For many of us, God has become a *subject* rather than a *person*, and we are constantly wrestling him onto a gurney so we can vivisect him, shushing him when he speaks, nodding and mumbling to ourselves, scrawling our observations into our little lined notebooks. As professors, we've set out the texts, made a list of banned books, pulled the shades, and locked the classroom door. We've handed out number two pencils and seated our students in alphabetical order and made sure they are quiet so they can hear the squeak of our pen on the whiteboard as we sketch out a diagram explaining, once and for all, "This is everything we know about the Holy Spirit."

As students, we are devout and dedicated but frankly a bit bored. We know all about the Holy Spirit and are ready for the next lesson. We listlessly turn the pages, glancing at the next chapter, wondering if there will be a quiz.

Paul J. Pastor is the wild-eyed, passionate, beloved professor who bursts into the classroom and shouts at his audience to put down their pencils and stand on their chairs. He's the life-changing, brilliant teacher we all wish we could have.

And this book—this gorgeous, transformative book—is a field trip.

Everyone loves to leave the classroom and get out in the real world, and Paul is a delightful, wise, and canny guide.

As if our whole lives we have studied the ocean in a windowless room, Paul herein packs us into a bus headed for the coast. We knew about salinity and tides, fissures and marine biology, ecology and a thousand other bits of trivia, but now Paul has us, pants rolled to our knees, wading in cool tide pools and touching the thick gelatinous edges of sea anemones. He shows us in this book that the ocean is not just something to know about, but a vast, beautiful, unchanging but varied, ancient yet always new, life-filled experience larger than ourselves.

He teaches us to love the sea.

Then he stands with us at the cliff's edge as the sun sets in the west, and we put our toes just over the edge, the sharp stone beneath our bare feet. He tells us that if we jump, we will feel the sting of the water as we enter, and then, beneath its surface, we will experience wonders: we will feel the currents and hear the distant mournful song of the whales, and we will see through filtered sunlight jungles of undulating seaweed and flashes of color as fish dart in and out of safety.

This book is not only a pilgrimage, not only a spiritual discipline, though it is those things. I've come to believe that in some sense it is not even a book. It is an invitation to dive into the deep presence of the Holy Spirit and to truly *know* him, not just know *about* him. Like the ocean, this book is full of vast peace, of hidden dangers, of wonders both small and great.

Don't rush through this book. Linger. Savor it. I wouldn't read more than one chapter a day, or maybe one chapter repeated each day for a week. Don't squeeze the knowledge from it; pause and speak to the Holy Spirit as you gracefully swim through it.

Again, one of the most important human activities is seeking to know God. Allow this book to accompany you in that activity. Allow Paul and this book to be part of your community as you seek to know the Holy Spirit well. I know of no better compliment than this: Paul's love for the Holy Spirit, as evidenced in these pages, is *contagious*.

Read on, and fall in love.

Matt Mikalatos
Author of *Sky Lantern* and *The First Time We Saw Him*

A FEW WORDS

Few elements of Christian life or theology are so underappreciated as the Holy Spirit. Many of us have no clear conception of who the Spirit is or how the Spirit works beyond our often-hazy gleanings from sermons and hymns. We cannot articulate how our spiritual lives are woven and empowered by the Spirit. Even though I came from a charismatic-leaning faith background, I found myself maturing in the Christian faith with many unanswered questions about and a deep yearning to know the Holy Spirit.

But for many years he stayed a mystery.

As I progressed through high school faith, college theological studies, seminary, ministry, and into my career, I found myself returning again and again to these questions: *Who is the Spirit? Where is the Spirit in my life?* I learned all the "right" theological answers, but they did not *live* as I felt they should. Every so often the Spirit became visible indirectly, like a dark bird who moves in a dark tree, only to disappear again. The enigma remained.

I cannot point to a single moment of clarity, but in the manner of many searchers realizing that what they were looking for was there all along, I began to feel that I had been allowed to pierce the mystery. I began to see the truth.

Where was the Spirit, but in my life all along! The Spirit's presence did not require my recognition to be utterly real. I had missed seeing the Spirit in the everyday—in the colors of water, the eyes of a child, my daily work, my daily bread. I began to realize that only through embracing the Spirit's immanence—his intimate presence in all of creation—would I be able to make any kind of *lived* sense of him; to *know* him like I know a lover and friend; to understand the rich teaching about him; to see his power as elemental, delicate, unshakable, the inner life of all love and existence, of me and of you. He was a mystery more than ever, but an open one, like birth or astronomy.

This book is a tracing of that lived mystery—a dive, open-eyed, from flashes and sparks of my own journey into the great life of God's Spirit around us, into the face of the deep, the watery abyss of creation, the nothing that somehow contained everything there ever was and would be. This dive ripples out in personal story; rambling rabbit runs of thought, history, and theology; musings on the arts; musings on nature; snippets of pretty close to everything in the world, which I am discovering to be a place utterly *full* of the Spirit of God.

This is not an exhaustive work on the doctrine of the Holy Spirit, but neither is it strictly devotional. This is a diver's belt woven of fourteen strands, each a biblically grounded personal essay centering on a particular aspect of the Spirit's person and work. With whatever you find true and beautiful here, I hope you'll reflect on the Spirit's work in your own life.

I chose to arrange the book in two pairs of seven to help organize and visualize the movement of the Spirit throughout the Bible. These are inspired by Spirit-related symbols from the book of Revelation. The "seven stars" of part 1 are key passages from the Old Testament about the person and work of the Holy Spirit. The "seven lampstands" of part 2 are key passages from the Greek Scriptures of the New Testament. (These passages are not about what the seven lampstands symbolize in their original use in the book of Revelation.) Believing that thinking of the Spirit as an impersonal "it" is a greater misstep than the by no means fully accurate "he" (God is spoken of with both masculine and feminine imagery in the Bible), I have gone with the latter.

The Spirit's glorious mystery is a *journey*, one that encompasses and sanctifies all that we encounter. As we grow in our ability to receive the Spirit's life, he infuses ours from both within and beyond us, leading us to the Father and the Son, painting our whole world with joy, color, and the love we were made for.

In knowing him, our lives are transformed.

I pray that you find this book inspiring to your imagination and good for your soul. Please read it in the spirit I offer it—with humility, joy, and a heart turned ever toward the Fire.

Part 1
SEVEN STARS

✳ ✳ ✦ ✸ ✸ ✳ ✳

THE FACE OF THE DEEP
Knowing the Spirit Who Creates

The quest for faith is a lunar endeavor,
not warmer and brighter, but darker and wetter.
—Five O'Clock People, "Lunar"

In a very low voice, a whisper, it says ... "I am
what there is before there is anything there."
—Liniers, *What There Is Before There Is Anything There*

In the beginning God created the heaven and the earth. And the earth
was without form, and void; and darkness was upon the face of the
deep. And the Spirit of God moved upon the face of the waters.
—Genesis 1:1–2 (KJV)

Once, on a bitterly cold Oregon autumn night, a friend and I took flashlights to a nearby lake. I was sixteen, eager for an adventure, and a midnight swim sounded like a good idea.

It was raining in great gray peels—the air was heavy as canvas. There were no stars, no hints of stars, no moon, no reflection from any tree or blade of grass. Noises from the woods were muted and disorienting. Everything smelled like nothing. We walked to the end of a slimy black dock, shivering, trying to act excited. We counted to three, then ran shirtless and barefoot off the dock as rain hissed into the lake. For a breathless moment I hung there in the rain, in the water above that fell into the water below, that place between the dive and the splash.

Then I came down.

All was seamless, suffocating night. I could not tell if my eyes were open or closed as the frigid water swallowed me. It must have been only fifty degrees. Heavy, clinging things (weeds, I hoped) swirled around my legs. In shock from the temperature, I screamed out underwater, great involuntary bubbles, and for an awful moment I was there— back at the very beginning, back under the face of the deep.

A second is as a thousand years to a person underwater, particularly if that person is me, adolescent, in a midnight lake. It is dark under the face of the deep, dark beyond description, because light is unknown there. It is a place where the rules of gravity and charity and depth and knowing and being don't exist. There is no up or sideways or down, only rumors of waves, and a wind above them, some infinity away.

Everyone in the world has asked where we all came from. Have you ever lain beneath a night spattered with stars, wondering whether you and the constellations share a maker? Have you ever felt your pulse, felt your breathing at some random time, only to be prompted to wonder for what reason your veins throb and your lungs fill and empty over and over again? Have you wondered at a mountain, at a tide pool, at a swelling twilight city?

One way or another, we all have.

To matter at all, every great story must start at the same place: the beginning. And the beginning is dark and wild. All over the world people hush their friends in the circle around the fire and start off the grand old tales in the same way:

"In the beginning there was nothing—no earth, no living beings. There were only darkness, water, and Cyclone, the wind,"[1] say the Jicarilla Apaches.

"In the beginning not anything existed,"[2] wrote Icelander Snorri Sturluson in *The Prose Edda*.

"The earth began as nothing but water and darkness,"[3] the Cherokee know.

"In the beginning there was no earth, no day or night, and not even time itself,"[4] the Mossi say.

"The world at first was endless space in which existed only the Creator,"[5] say the Hopi people.

As the Wichita tell it, "In the beginning there were neither sun, nor stars, nor anything else that we know today."[6]

"Long, long ago, when heaven and earth were still one … all the matter of the universe swirled chaotically,"[7] says *The Classic of Mountains and Seas* of the Chinese, a book already ancient when Rome rose.

And of course, the Hebrews: "In the beginning God created the heaven and the earth" (Gen. 1:1 KJV).

Translator Everett Fox nearly manages to capture in English the rush and lilting cadence of the Hebrew text:

> At the beginning of God's creating
> of the heavens and the earth,
> when the earth was wild and waste,
> darkness over the face of Ocean,
> rushing-spirit of God hovering over the face of the waters.[8]

The original Hebrew word for "spirit" is רוּחַ (*ruach*)—the same word used for the wind, for the life-breath of God's creatures, and for the inner spirit of humans. It is a simple, everyday word.

"Wild and waste." *Tohu wa bohu*, goes the Hebrew.

Formless. Void.

We can't understand the light of presence without the darkness of absence. Consider the abyss. How can we, so used to a world teeming with light and living things, imagine the vacuum with which our world began? How can we imagine the early emptiness, the wild waves of the Bible's first words?

WE CAN'T UNDERSTAND THE LIGHT OF PRESENCE WITHOUT THE DARKNESS OF ABSENCE.

When we close our eyes to dive, to picture the birth of our world, we must open our imaginations. Do you hear the black, mad waves crashing, lapping against nothing? Do you feel the disorientation swallow you—the vacuum, the sudden cold, the ancient chaos, the embodiment of the most fearful sense of endless deep, of abyss, of black empty? Does nothingness touch you and make you cold? If we do not understand the abyss, we will not understand creation. It is dark but a very good place to start.

As many others have observed, it is the *who* of creation that these verses care about. That who is mentioned twice in these verses—first simply called "God," then referenced as the *ruach* of God—the wind of God, the breath of God, the "rushing spirit."

Out of formlessness, form was made. Out of chaos, order. Out of emptiness, filling. Out of barrenness, fruit. Out of the abyss, a place to stand, to know, to *be* by the power of the Spirit of God.

Christians believe that God exists eternally as a triune being—a truth I have often rattled off with neither understanding nor reverence. We are not unique in claiming that the Divine is more than one person. Neither are we unique in believing that there is only one god. But we are, at least as far as I am aware, unique in our stubborn persistence that the three persons we name as God somehow remain *one*.

Many of us are accustomed to thinking of the Trinity as an interesting theological accessory. Like the observation of a great whale that, while interesting to cetologists (people who study whales), has little bearing for land dwellers. Perhaps, we think, discussion of the triune nature of God, while interesting to theologians, has little to do with the spiritual life of humans.

But what if the triune nature of God is the great truth lying at the center of all creation, the very foundation of love and making and knowing and giving? So close to us as to be nearly invisible, for we have been made in its image?

Let's consider it. The Trinity is our great mystery of theology, at once attractive and repellent to human understanding. It is as if a math problem had been found whose sum was simultaneously correct and incorrect. No matter how many times we calculate it, it comes out wrong. And right. And wrong. It is an uncovering of an order so great that it nearly looks like chaos. It is something simple and beyond us.

From all eternity (which means outside of any concept of time or space in which beginnings and endings have any meaning at all), one God has existed in three persons, whom we are accustomed to calling Father, Son, and Holy Spirit.

No one has ever been able to speak of this God without resorting to metaphors, so we understand that even our very use of these terms is calculated not for accuracy but for the limitation of our inaccuracies.

GOD HAS ALWAYS BEEN PURE LOVE, PURE JOY, ONE DIVINITY IN THREE PERSONS: FATHER, SON, AND HOLY SPIRIT.

It is impossible for us to conceive of a father who did not exist before his child, but we must try to do so, for this is the first mystery of the Trinity. God the Father, without any "firstness," without any priority of time or importance, begets the Son eternally. So, then, what makes him a father if he did not come before the Son? This fact (itself a holy enigma): the Father loves the Son with a love that is paternal. The Father looks upon and gives to and begets and loves the Son from all eternity with the kind of love with which fathers love.

To compound the great mystery, it is likewise impossible for us to understand a Son who is in age, power, and nature equal to his

Father. Yet this is the nature of the second person of the Trinity, who is eternally generated from the Father yet without derivative second-ness, existing utterly outside of any limitation of time or space. What makes him the Son is this eternal begetting, and as a result, the Son looks upon and loves the Father from all eternity with the kind of love with which sons love their fathers.

And then there is the Holy Spirit. A clue rests in the very name, for "spirit" is another word for "breath," and the Spirit is breath. Again, our metaphors fail (for who can conceive of a breath that is itself a person equal in faculties and power to the ones who breathe it out?), but as the Father and the Son—both God, both perfect love—look upon one another, each loving the other according to their shared single nature and difference of person, they breathe out *love*, love that is itself a divine person, sharing fully in their nature and coeternal with them.

Theologians call this timeless breathing the *eternal procession of the Spirit*. And in this way, God has always been pure love, pure joy, one Divinity in three persons: Father, Son, and Holy Spirit. The relational foundation of everything.

Against many popular conceptions that picture God only as a receiver of adoration, love, and glory, the correct understanding of God's beautiful triune nature clearly illustrates that from all eternity he knows the totality of love and self-giving. There was never a time when the Father did not shower the Son with everything he was, never a time when the Son did not give all of himself in return, never a time when the Holy Spirit did not join, blessing and giving and reblessing and regiving, as the very breath of love. God, from before any beginning of begin-nings, was always the God who covenanted himself away, who poured himself limitlessly, who gave all and received all. Lover and Beloved.

God has never known a time when he himself did not dwell in the richness of relationship and community. He has always been a giver, always been a lover, always been part of a family, as it were. Always together.

He *is*, and that is to say, he is utter love, the giver of himself and the receiver of another. Thus, he was always himself, undivided, uncontained, uncontaminated, with no division or partition of nature, yet known to himself and to us as One in Three. Love, pure personal love beyond any richness of metaphor or imagination.

The Holy Spirit, the breath of love, is not an impersonal force or by-product of the Godhead. Sometimes the symbols that humanity has used to talk about God's Spirit (fire, dove, wind, breath, and holy oil are a few) can confuse us. But the Spirit is not merely a particular form that the one God takes when he wishes to relate to his creation in a particular way, nor is the Spirit somehow a second-class member of the Godhead (the errand-bird of Father and Son). The Spirit is a full and vibrant person because the Spirit is the eternal God, the Spirit both of the Father and of the Son, and as wholly God as either of the other two members of the Trinity.

The implication of the one God who exists as a unified three is this: from before time itself existed, *relationship* did. In the love of the Father, Son, and Spirit, joy has existed from eternity past. Admiration existed, pleasure existed, kindness and gentleness and wisdom existed. Camaraderie existed—with fun, commitment, good counsel, loyalty, and fellowship. This is a brilliant truth—all three persons of God clearly can be termed the Maker of the world. But the Spirit's connection to creation, by his immanence, the closeness that the oldest story tells us he kept with the face of the deep and all that lay below it, is something particularly precious.

THE IMPLICATION OF THE ONE GOD WHO EXISTS AS A UNIFIED THREE IS THIS: FROM BEFORE TIME ITSELF EXISTED, RELATIONSHIP DID.

We all were made in the glorious image of the one whose very nature is love, perfect and resplendent.

In my most rational moments, the doctrine of the Trinity is delectable torture. In my most worshipful moments, it is a glorious, personal joy—a mystery of faith prompting us to contemplate and adore. At every moment it is a reminder that no one is ever alone, and that community, love, and belonging are not simply cosmic aberrations but the root nature of reality.

But to be fully welcomed into this love, it helps to know the Lover.

Of the three persons of the Trinity, the Spirit's person and work are the most difficult to grasp. Why is this? Two reasons, I think.

First, the person of the Spirit is usually described with impersonal images. How does Scripture talk about the Spirit? As wind, as breath, as fire, as a dove (birds are not typically known for their godlike qualities).

Through vague relational roles: the "helper," the "comforter." And in his relationship to Christ (Acts 16:7 uses "the Spirit of Jesus").

It is difficult to imagine having a personal relationship with the blazing fire of Pentecost, with the dove descending on Jesus, or with the breeze that "blows where it chooses" (John 3:8). I lack the experience, the imaginative capacity for it, real and potent though it may be.

Because of such unfamiliarity, confusion over the Spirit's work takes many forms. He represents unpredictability to some—a mystic strangeness. At worst, the Spirit, if misunderstood, can easily be weaponized, name-dropped, leveraged, or falsely used to abuse and silence.

While we may lack the language to describe the person of the Spirit accurately or to speak of his specific work, he is the member of the Trinity most intimately involved with every turning of our life and world. He is our intercessor, who groans, the apostle Paul said, for the church before the Father with words unutterable. "The Spirit of Jesus," as Acts calls him, filled our inmost selves when we were born again. The vital, invisible, spiritually tangible works of baptism, filling, sealing, and sanctification? They are all through the activity of the Spirit applying the life of the resurrected Christ, by the will and power of the Father, to our lives. He is the personal love of the triune God made most intimate for his people.

And all this—even the most personal good that God works on our behalf—is an extension of that first great breath of creation, grounded in the Trinity. He is the creator of the "very good," and it shows, even now, though we often fail to see it. Our lives, our spiritual growth, any development of strength or beauty or wonder that we may attain, is the continuing creation (marred though our world has become) that the Spirit still performs and sustains—and shall, for eternity.

All is still dark. The wind over the water ruffles like feathers. In the moment of creation, all will explode with light and flourishing life, pouring out, awash over moments and endless eons, cascading out of God's good will and perfect power. But now all is quiet, waiting. Silent before the ultimate storm.

But when the work above the deep is finished, over it all will be said these words: "Good. Very good."

In water our world was made, and in water we were made—entering the world from darkness and the secret waters of our mother into the light.

My wife, Emily, and I have three children, two of whom were born in the water. I will never forget those long hours of labor through the day and the night, or the feeling of buoyancy, of *returning* that entering the water during childbirth meant to us. The water brought relief from pain for my wife, brought both warmth and coolness, brought a sense of peace in the moments of panic that labor brings to new parents. The water gave us its own gifts during our times of needful joy.

And isn't this reminder of beginnings the elemental nature of water—of the ocean and every river that feeds it? This is our symbol of creation and re-creation, birth and baptism. There is a reminder of the primal deep in every pool after the rain, in every glass of water from the municipal tap, in the pools of birth, in artesian wells, in the steam from a shrieking kettle, in the salt sting of storms on the sea. Even in our bodies, which are about 60 percent water, we have the ancient reminder—creation lives *here*—in this flesh, in the very clots of our wounds, in our tears, in the wet kiss of a child.

The abyss, whether formed or unformed, is never far away.
The water still surrounds, dark and deep and good.

In our present state of fallen humanity, we have lost our vision for a world utterly founded on love. But the need, the call, the root yearning is there. It has been made to be there. But what is this love?

The German Catholic philosopher Josef Pieper, in *About Love,* sums up all of this (all of everything, really) beautifully. What is love? Pieper thinks it is a very simple thing—to look on another and say, "It's good that you are; how wonderful that you exist!"[9]

What is love? Not defining others by their function, by what they can give to anyone. But looking on others with nothing in the heart save the original utterance of the Beloved: "And … it was very good" (Gen. 1:31). What is love? The Father looking on the Son looking on the Spirit looking on the Father, all saying with one voice, "It is good that you are here." What is love? The Trinity is love. What is love? The Spirit hovering over the face of the deep, rustling the waters, looking at reflections laughing back from the glorious abyss. What is love? God placing his image on humanity and willing that we should give and receive love in the manner he does, lavishly and for eternity. What is love? The darkness and the light, the sun, moon, and stars, day and night, the trees and vegetation, the birds and fish, the mammals and reptiles, all creeping things, women and men, all of the vast "very good." We are love.

We come from love, we go to love, and any other conception of the cosmos is a bitter lie.

Creation is love, and the Creator is our Lover. God is love, and so the Spirit is love, and in creating and sustaining us, he loves us in the most specific of possible ways—numbering our hairs, maintaining the existence of our constituent molecules, manifesting his presence in every joy and grief we experience. Giving us form, being, and duration. Knowing us. Being known by us.

We are given the beginning of our story.

This is the first star, a priceless, shining gift from the Spirit.

WE COME FROM LOVE, WE GO TO LOVE, AND ANY OTHER CONCEPTION OF THE COSMOS IS A BITTER LIE.

Once, above the unformed black abyss, the Spirit of God hovered. And there above the unknowable waves, he whispered eternal love to the Father, to the Son, to the face of the deep. He whispered eternal love to you, to me, to all of the "very good."

Whether you know it or not, whether you have ever felt it or heard it personally for yourself, we have all had the holy words spoken over us: *"It's good that you are; how wonderful that you exist!"* The Spirit has never stopped saying this to each and all of us.

His love for you is infinite. He gives and gives and gives himself. He calls to us from above the surface of the water. Calls us to come to him.

To matter at all, you and I and every one of God's children must start at the same place: the beginning.

Can you hear the Spirit's voice now, echoing out across the waters?

TOOLING THE CREATORS
Making with the Spirit Who Inspires

How can my muse want subject to invent,
While thou dost breathe, that pour'st into my verse
Thine own sweet argument?
—William Shakespeare, "Sonnet 38"

Then Moses said to the people of Israel, "See, the LORD has
called by name Bezalel the son of Uri, son of Hur, of the
tribe of Judah; and he has filled him with the Spirit of God,
with skill, with intelligence, with knowledge, and with all
craftsmanship.... And he has inspired him to teach."
—Exodus 35:30–31, 34 (ESV)

I think the Holy Ghost has written not only the Bible, but all books.
—George Bernard Shaw

This is rather hard on the Holy Ghost.
—Jorge Luis Borges, *This Craft of Verse*

The second deepest canyon in the United States is the Salmon River canyon in western Idaho. I spent a summer in college there once, living under a tarp on a white sand beach and rafting the roaring whitewater with students who came with church groups. We rode the same stretch of water daily for weeks, surging and shouting with the rabid foam and browning like sage in the sun. The canyon is in a land of moose and rattlesnakes, abandoned silver mines and mountain sheep, fragrant Ponderosa pines, and the glittered splash of trout.

The canyon is deep in the homeland of the Nez Perce people, whose ancient trails, when the light is right, may be seen from far away, snaking up the hills surrounding the river, though I dare you to find them when you're trying to. One day, after a great run down the river, we were pulling out our rafts on a pebbled beach, and as I waited for our vans to come and load up our boats, something caught my eye. Nature, it's been said, doesn't make straight lines, and eyes grown accustomed to the wilderness see clean edges as stark as if they were painted red.

THE MADE THING HELD SOMETHING OF ITS MAKER IN IT.

I turned and crouched.

An old arrowhead! I placed it on my palm.

A tiny triangle, point and barbs knapped expertly from a piece of moss agate, still sharp enough to cut. It was small—the smallest I'd ever seen up close, but as clean as if it were new. The size made me think it was made for a child's bow; the point would be dwarfed by any adult's arrow. The agate was lovely, bone colored and barely opaque—an unnecessary flair of beauty if it were merely for hunting small game. It shone when held before the sun. I laid it on my palm and felt for a moment a bright connection with its maker.

We were so different, I and the one who had created this thing, and yet we had so much in common. We were both born in this northwestern land, though to different peoples and in different centuries. We had both dipped and splashed and bathed in the waters of this river, though we surely called it by different names. We had each seen the phases of the moon pass in light and darken the canyon hills and the Sawtooth Mountains beyond. I was an archer too, though I had learned on a compound bow of modern composite, hung with oblong wheels and loosing spring-loaded steel arrowheads. Its maker was probably a man, thus a son, likely a brother, a member of a clan and a family. He told jokes. He wept. He wondered what his people would remember him for. Wondered what God was like. But how different too—the pinnacle of technology for him was the repeating rifle, the training of Appaloosas, the old traditional crafts of knapping flint, of weaving. Technology for me was the GPS, the automobile, the electric light, the cell phone, Predator drones, the Internet.

Through this tiny arrowhead, I could almost glimpse him.

The made thing held something of its maker in it.

Humans are innate creators. There is no place we go in the world that we don't leave our mark—the mark of human culture. Craft and creativity are as impossible to separate from the human experience as worship or friendship. Whatever our branch of endeavor, concrete or abstract, it's impossible for us not to make meaning—impossible, in our own small way, not to call things up, like the Spirit, from the unformed place below the face of the deep.

From here the work of all humans inevitably flows together to become the work of making and maintaining cultures—our foods, our ways of being, our arts and crafts, our memories, our songs, the pictures and tools and everything else we create. But it's easy sometimes to get so caught up in the making (which in daily life for most of us is less than glamorous) that we don't think much about the meaning of the making.

ALL THIS WORK OF CREATING AND MAKING, I BELIEVE, IS SACRED WORK, THE SPIRIT'S ORIGINAL SACRED WORK CONTINUING IN AND THROUGH US.

The Spirit of God creates through human hands too, directed by the mind and imagination of a creator. In the story of the Exodus, a man named Bezalel, "filled" and "inspired" by the Spirit of God, led Israel's people to worship through his skill to make things. The Bible doesn't speak of what this filling and inspiration specifically meant, but more detail might only have confused the point. From the prominence that the writer of Exodus gives to Bezalel's apparently less-than-miraculous qualities (skill, intelligence, knowledge, craftsmanship), it's easy to infer that the Spirit didn't miraculously grant what this man needed to fulfill his calling—rather, the Spirit met things present already and used them to extend his call of love via the hand of the creator through his culture and into the world.

We are not told if Bezalel was a young man or old. Scripture says next to nothing about his background. We are told what is relevant to the story—he was a creator without peer in Israel, a maker of unusual expertise. He was skilled to pass his "inspiration" on to others—not only to do but to teach how to do. For the newly wandering Hebrew culture, he embodied the pinnacle of art and skill at that moment, the pinnacle of their ability to manufacture the materials for God's tent of meeting.

Bezalel had *skill*, what was needed to get the job done; *intelligence*, an innate gifting that can't be taught or bought; *knowledge*, learned ability; and *craftsmanship*, the ability to excellently execute and produce. To make imagined things *real*.

All this work of creating and making, I believe, is sacred work, the Spirit's original sacred work continuing in and through us.

The great Peruvian writer Mario Vargas Llosa wrote in *Letters to a Young Novelist* that his vocation—writing fiction—was a form of dissent, "rebellion," the product of "dissatisfaction" with "life as it is."[1] He said that the novelist's calling is to reimagine the world, to make a new and better place to be human. Is the world too harsh, too cruel, too apathetic, too filled with vice and malice and avarice? Write a new one, said Llosa. The great work of a novelist's life is saying no to the ways that life has gone wrong, channeling the deep dissatisfaction with our broken reality, the dissent that we all have felt, into the creation of fictions that speak of worlds that perhaps are kinder than our own, or perhaps only better about interpreting their cruelty for us to understand.

Fortunately for our race, this is the Spirit's work as well as the novelist's. But the story God is writing is not fictional. The necessity of this comes from the story of sin and death told in Genesis 3, where our earliest parents rejected the path of God for their own path, a path that walked away from love, from creation, from harmony and relationship. A path that walked away from the very good.

I am slowly learning that the fall of humanity, prompted by our twisted original dissatisfaction with life as it was before the brokenness of sin and spiritual death, impacted our world more deeply than we could begin to describe. We were dissatisfied with life as it was, and through our sin we marred—and still mar—the world. Up from below the face of the deep, the Spirit called all things in love, but the brokenness of sin, of self-love, of broken faith took the "very good" of the original called ones and bent them, tainted them, soured them in the stomach.

We marred the world. We have done it in every generation our race has run over the earth. Look around. We mar our neighbors, mar our land, mar our relationships. We mar our parents and our children, our animals, our cultures. We mar those who are different than we are. We mar those who are the same. We are wounders, perverse and contrary, selfish, petty, cruel.

We forget the wonder of creation, the goodness of the Spirit's words of love.

We forget the life over the water.

But we who mar can, by the Spirit, remake. There is no area of human endeavor—from leading nations to sweeping streets—that cannot be "inspired" as an act of dissent against the world as it is. While some, like Bezalel, might receive a special dose of inspiration, we all have been made in the image of the Great Maker.

Like arrowheads, we hold so much of our Maker in us.

What is the great work of Bezalel, of you, of me, of humanity? Joining that Spirit who not only made but now *dissents* against the marring of his "very good." The work of our lives is reimagining the world with God. This is a return to the real—a past real barely remembered, a future real barely imagined.

THERE IS NO AREA OF HUMAN ENDEAVOR— FROM LEADING NATIONS TO SWEEPING STREETS—THAT CANNOT BE "INSPIRED."

I am beginning to learn my own call to this. And I am finding that the great creative work of my life, known by the moments when I burn most truly *alive* as a maker, are not always the ones that I expect. Creative work is not only the visible, the glorious, the obvious. It is also in the things I am not so great at or that aren't so glamorous—in the crafting of leather, in gardening, in chopping the wood that heats our home in winter. In my unexpected spiritual discipline of doing the family dishes at night. In child rearing.

The call to the good rebellion of the Spirit comes *everywhere*.

Through the ringing of hammers and the *shush* of weavers, Bezalel lived out his calling, crafting the tent God chose to travel in as he wandered with Israel, the utensils of worship, the blue hangings of the tabernacle (echoing the sky above), the lampstands that flickered before the mercy seat, and the holy bread of the tent's table.

No matter what our specific calling, no matter what degree of skill in vocation or occupation we possess, what knowledge we have obtained, what intelligence we were born with, what craftsmanship we exercise, we are made to make. Whatever our position, role, challenges, resources, or lack of any of these, we are called by the Spirit of God, full of love and power, to re-create the world.

Are we powerful in work—like Bezalel—in the world's eyes? Are we full of skill, good gifts, and the qualities that people notice? We must follow the Spirit, choosing humility and service, and using our gifts for the worship of God, the service of his people, and the wider good of our peoples and places.

Are we forgotten in the eyes of the world? Do we lack education, choice of career, meaningful or dignified labor, fair compensation? The Spirit, Maker of makers, sees our talents and has gifted us uniquely to help him change the world—even if that change is invisible now, hidden like an arrowhead on a beach of stones.

"Whatever your hand finds to do, do with your might," the Preacher said in chapter 9 of the book of Ecclesiastes (v. 10). But what if our hand can find nothing to do for a wage, wasted in the dullness of a wasteful world system that allows for "unemployment"? We should work for good without a wage, knowing that the Spirit sees contribution, not compensation, as the mark of a craftsperson in his likeness. If we cannot work at all because of one condition or another? Then we must speak (to any who will listen) truth, encouragement, and peace, and remembrance of the day of re-creation that is coming. Are we unable to speak? Then we must pray and intercede with silent inner groanings, knowing that the Spirit does the same before the Father, pleading on our behalf.

WE ARE MAKERS, DISSENTERS, REIMAGINERS. JUST LIKE THE SPIRIT WHO MADE US.

By none of these statements do I mean to make light of the challenges we face in our labor. But in the shadowed world, I think the Spirit means to make Light of them.

You and I and the Nez Perce arrow maker and every member of the human family are beloved children of God, called up, makers made in his image, brilliant little masterpieces of creation. We are makers, dissenters, reimaginers. Just like the Spirit who made us.

Bezalel's fire of inspiration is our fire. The Spirit who inspires the hand of the worker is not merely a footnote in a dusty Bible tale. The Spirit who empowered him empowers us—for making, for beauty, for creativity, for craft, for stewardship, for production, for faithful use of our gifts in service to God, in service to the people of God, in service to the whole cosmos.

The star set in the old creator's palm can be set in yours as well, a little sun, an engine of life and love. It really can be.

You may even know when it is.

I sat over coffee one day with Jim, a famous sculptor in my city. His bronzework ripples with life and musculature, taking life to a place of cast permanence, solid and iconic. He sat under a portrait of Crazy Horse in east Portland's Bipartisan Café (*"Where Partisans Go for Pie!"*), and the rain outside fell as loud as if it were made of metal.

Jim told me the story of seeing his first sculpture. He was out to see a film or something with his father. They got hungry. Sitting in a diner, Jim picked a piece of chewing gum off the seat. Rather than chide, his father took the clump, smiled, and fashioned it into a boat. In that moment, Jim learned that clay can become anything.

"You use a medium," he told me, "any medium to *see* another, to *know* another, and finally, to *show* yourself what you have understood."

At the time, he'd recently completed a project that took him to the streets, where he asked the homeless to pose for him. He sculpted their busts from clay, honored the lines and contours of their individual heads, and displayed their lovely likenesses in a fine gallery to indict the empire that bustled about them every day with little care and even less seeing. When I asked why he thought it was easier for people like me to see the homeless in clay than in flesh, his only reply was a wry smile.

To see, to know, to understand. These are ways of talking around a central thing, of talking about a simple word that undergirds them all. You know what it is.

Love. The artist, the craftsperson, the worker, whatever the choice of medium or subject, whatever the field of industry or endeavor, is a continuation of the Spirit's original "very good."

The made thing holds something of its maker in it.

John Ruskin began his mighty little monograph *On Art and Life* by pronouncing Gothic the most "moral" architectural style.[2] You may laugh at the application of moral categories to building design, but Ruskin will talk you out of it. His argument is that any architectural style that suppresses the wild, creative imperfections of craftspeople in favor of the polished, "perfect" vision of a single master architect is immoral, inhuman, anti-Christian in its insistence on uniformity over the sacredness of individual expression. The Gothic, with its wild stonework, its brilliant crudities, allows for chips, for chisel marks, for the work of *humans*. Real people. You and me.

The Spirit's work of continuing creation would have been much cleaner if he'd merely done it all himself. But *clean* is not the ultimate goal of making—*love* is. And so the world of possibilities, of cultures, flourishes outward, every trail made by the heels of its walkers. Some of us shudder to think that we leave footprints.

Others vandalize and mar the way. But we *all* are called to reimagine the world.

Like Bezalel, filled with the Spirit and blooming into a holy maker after the image of God himself, we are called, gifted, asked to imagine, to dissent from the marred world as it is. We are invited to join the Spirit in re-creating the world, one brick, one novel, one child, one burrito at a time.

And how beautiful this is!

WE ALL ARE CALLED TO REIMAGINE THE WORLD.

How beautiful the healing of wounds, the building of cities, the telling of stories with the imagination of God! How beautiful the raising and teaching of children; how beautiful the bridge builders, the carpenters, the plumbers, the cooks! How beautiful the blowing of glass, the raising of sheep and cattle; the farmers, the doctors, the nurse's assistants; those who make arrows, who edit, who paint. The arborists, the tollbooth collectors, the poets, the pastors, the missionaries, the counselors, the farmhands, the roadside produce vendors, the newspaper hawkers, the roofers, the gardeners, the coders, the fashion designers, the hotel maids, the engineers, the stonemasons, the ecologists, the physicists, the toy makers, the repairers of roads! Those who laugh over their work, those who weep over their work; how beautiful is Christ, who "plays in ten thousand places"![3] How beautiful the Spirit whose breath fires the mind!

How beautiful, how beautiful, how beautiful!

How beautiful on every mountain are the feet of every one of us, who with head and heart and hands brings the good news. And how endlessly beautiful is this mystery: *we* who've been made hold so much of our Maker in us, the Spirit of life and love and creation.

How can our muse want subject to invent?

THE POWER OF PROPHETS
Embracing the Spirit Who Speaks Truth

The Holy Spirit sanctifies and transforms all that he touches.
—Cyril of Jerusalem

*He pours contempt on princes, and makes
them wander in trackless wastes … all
wickedness will shut its mouth.*
—Psalm 107: Part II, verses 40, 42,
The Book of Common Prayer

Therefore it is said, "Is Saul also among the prophets?"
—1 Samuel 19:24

If you open a map of Oregon, you might after considerable searching find the tiny town of Antelope east of the Warm Springs Reservation, deep in the heart of Wasco County. "Population: 46" says the 2010 Census,[1] and driving on Antelope's gritty main drag, you wonder if they've padded that number with jackrabbits. You've heard about ghost towns? Antelope is a ghost town, just one that hasn't realized that it has died, still shuffling about its routine, humming a tune that skips like a scratched Gene Autry record:

Back in the saddle again ...
Back in the saddle again ...
Back in the saddle again ...

Much of what maintains the illusion of life in Antelope (other than the few kind, dry residents who pop up to sell soda to drivers on the Shaniko-Fossil Highway) is the town's proximity to a sprawling youth camp off to the southeast. When I was in college, our school held an annual retreat there—classes would shutter as students loaded up in their beater college cars, and we all caravanned to the ranch, where swimming pools and zip lines distracted us from our studies back in Portland. We tanned in the high desert sun, slept in apartment-style dormitories, ate in a mess hall larger than our gym, and hiked gritty trails that looked down on a sprawling compound of sidewalks and broad buildings.

"Ranch" falls short—this was a whole small town of a property. A beautiful, peaceful place.

But there is a strange story behind the land, one of the most bizarre tales in Oregon's history. Long before it was a Christian camp, the ranch—and sixty-four thousand acres surrounding it—was purchased in 1981 by the followers of "sex guru" Chandra Mohan Jain, alias Bhagwan Shree Rajneesh, who came to Oregon from Pune, India, with deep pockets and a vision for enlightenment.

Enlightenment meant many things to Rajneesh, including Rolls-Royces (ninety-three of them), sixty milligrams of Valium a day, and extremely free ideas about sexuality.[2] Enlightenment meant power.

Thousands of followers flocked to him, sheep to an indulgent shepherd. Within a few years, the colossal compound of Rancho

Rajneesh had bloated into "Rajneeshpuram," a town of more than two thousand people—complete with fire department, rifle-toting militia, and its own zip code.

But rural Oregon's zoning laws are strict, and Rajneesh's utopia of sex, drugs, and higher consciousness wasn't up to code. Frustrated in attempts at further expansion, the kindly facade of Rajneesh's entourage eroded. Political influence was tried, and failed, followed by more direct action.

The efforts to build heaven on earth became hellish. Poisonings, sloppy arson, and political manipulation were tried and failed. Busloads of homeless men were brought in to sway a local election with their purchased votes, then (when they began to be a nuisance) were served sedative-laced kegs of beer to knock them out before hauling them to be abandoned in nearby towns. And finally, in the largest bioterror attack on US soil, they used salmonella poison (home-brewed in a little cabin up one of the ranch's many canyons), maliciously infecting many citizens of The Dalles to the north.

Finally, madly, the prophet-king's dream collapsed. Rajneesh was deported and returned to India, where he died within a few years. But he left his mark in the canyons near Antelope, where his twisted truths built twisting roads that still snake off into the hills where I ran in a tie-dyed T-shirt under crackling pop music from '80s-era loudspeakers that once broadcast the voice of a false prophet who built a strange kingdom in the desert of Oregon.

What is prophecy? Who is a prophet?

Many of us picture someone like Elijah, a man tousled by the wilderness, weathered and strong like a Joshua tree, preaching ruin to the evil elite. Perhaps we see Deborah, a woman unignorable, whispering her messages to Barak in the breeze before battle with the enemies of God's people—smiling a bit when she sees (beyond natural sight) that it is a woman's hand that will bring victory. "The road on which you are going will not lead to your glory," she says into the war chief's ear, "for the LORD will sell Sisera into the hand of a woman" (Judg. 4:9).

But prophecy, the Spirit's speaking uniquely through human minds and lips, is not primarily about the future at all. It is a very specific speaking: the Spirit revealing God's fierce way of love in the face of the worldly powers that seek to destroy the "very good" of his creation.

We think of the prophets primarily as spokespeople, chanters of mysteries, human indicators of divine signs and seasons. The mouthpieces of God. And so they are, beyond a doubt. We picture them as people of inordinate power—after all, in the old stories they (by God's might) parted seas, raised the dead, made iron float, out-ran chariots, held the rain back, called the rain up, told the future, recalled the past, looked upon God himself.

People of power, yes—but in noting the power with which they move, we must never forget the weaknesses that highlight it. The great prophet Moses claimed a speech impediment. David's prophecies came not with the power of fire or wind, but with the weakness of song lyrics, the gentle thrum of a homemade harp. Anna, the prophetess in Luke 2, is a widow from girlhood, a very old woman who has spent her life in prayer, likely passed by those around her with little consideration. *The old widow*, they think. To be respected, mildly pitied. But she spoke wonders of the Christ child. Miriam, the slave-born sister of Moses, and leprous with jealousy, is a prophet too, as is Balaam, a seer-for-hire who spoke the truth with a grudge, to the frustration of his employer, who wanted to hire curses called on God's people. When the stone-smashing moments, the river-parting moments, the floating-ax moments happen in Scripture, they happen in a context of rather remarkable unremarkability.

WHAT ARE WE TO MAKE OF A SPIRIT WHO, OF ALL THE WAYS OF COMMUNICATION POSSIBLE IN A DIVINE IMAGINATION, CHOOSES TO VEIL WORDS IN RIDDLES?

We have questions about ancient prophecies and the persistence of prophetic words and giftings in our own day. I myself have had "prophecies" uttered over me—some I felt to be true, some baseless, and some too enigmatic to tell. What do we make of these things? And further, what are we to make of a Spirit who, of all the ways of communication possible in a divine imagination, chooses to veil words in riddles, signs acted out, and the flaws and weaknesses of such a strange and outcast bunch of women and men?

The prophet's role, typified by the prophetic writings of the Hebrew Bible, was to speak specifically and directly on God's behalf.

These clear and unmistakable speakings for God make up an overwhelming part of the Bible. In the Tanakh, the Jewish form of the Old Testament, the bulky middle section of the holy book is dedicated to the *Nevi'im*—the Prophets—which includes the narrative books of Joshua, Judges, Samuel, and Kings; all the "latter prophets," Isaiah, Jeremiah, Ezekiel; and the Book of the Twelve (the so-called minor prophets).

Mighty is the weight of these works—in the hand by bulk of page and ink, and in the heart by their beauty and ferocity. They are words that have brought down kingdoms and built them, that have comforted exiles, discomforted rulers, and haunted the imaginations and hearts of countless millions. They are the words of the prophets. Prophecy.

What is prophecy? The holy words of one who speaks for God. But who speaks for God?

Let's turn to the story of Saul, first king of Israel, and his unnerving encounter with the Spirit of prophecy. Here are the key portions of the text in 1 Samuel 19 from the New Revised Standard Version:

> Saul spoke with his son Jonathan and with all his servants about killing David. But ... Jonathan spoke well of David to his father Saul, saying to him, "The king should not sin against his servant David, because he has not sinned against you,

and because his deeds have been of good service to you.... Why then will you sin against an innocent person by killing David without cause?" Saul heeded the voice of Jonathan; Saul swore, "As the LORD lives, he shall not be put to death." ...

Then an evil spirit from the LORD came upon Saul, as he sat in his house with his spear in his hand, while David was playing music. Saul sought to pin David to the wall with the spear; but he eluded Saul, so that he struck the spear into the wall. David fled and escaped that night.

Saul sent messengers to David's house to keep watch over him, planning to kill him in the morning....

David fled and escaped; he came to Samuel at Ramah, and told him all that Saul had done to him. He and Samuel went and settled at Naioth.... Then Saul sent messengers to take David. When they saw the company of the prophets in a frenzy, with Samuel standing in charge of them, the spirit of God came upon the messengers of Saul, and they also fell into a prophetic frenzy. When Saul was told, he sent other messengers, and they also fell into a frenzy. Saul sent messengers again the third time, and they also fell into a frenzy. Then he himself went to Ramah. He came to the great well that is in Secu; he asked, "Where are Samuel and David?" And someone said, "They are at Naioth

in Ramah." He went there, toward Naioth in
Ramah; and the spirit of God came upon him. As
he was going, he fell into a prophetic frenzy, until
he came to Naioth in Ramah. He too stripped off
his clothes, and he too fell into a frenzy before
Samuel. He lay naked all that day and all that
night. Therefore it is said, "Is Saul also among the
prophets?" (vv. 1, 4–6, 9–11, 18, 20–24)

Fearing that his popular (and innocent) young son-in-law David
has designs on his throne, Saul, utterly corrupted by power, plans
David's death. Three times he attempts it. The first time, Saul is
persuaded by his son Jonathan to spare David's life. In the second
(omitted for length above), David slips away, as Saul's daughter
Michal tricks the royal hit men with an idol covered in goat hair and
stuffed under David's bedclothes.

And then the third—and the most bizarre: Saul's assassins track
David to the village of Naioth, where a whole group of prophets
live under the leadership of Samuel. (The Bible doesn't say enough
about their group to satisfy our questions.) While Jonathan inter-
ceded for David the first time, and Michal the second, the Spirit
blocks the blades of the killers the third time. They are overcome
not by persuasion or trickery but by the sheer overflow of what some
commentators can only term prophetic "frenzy." They are unable to
complete the murder. Saul sends two more bands. They each meet
the same fate, apparently shrinking Saul's pool of assassins while
swelling the ranks of the prophets.

Then Saul, no doubt breathing triple the murder he had commanded, decides that to kill some people right, you must do it yourself. He comes to Naioth. He picks up the trail. He follows it. He is undone.

Completely undone.

He goes from breath of murder, of power consolidation, to the breath of *God*. Saul joins the company of the prophets. In the glory of the words, he strips himself naked. He lies on the ground. There, before Samuel, the very man who raised him up and anointed him king over a young land, he grovels, ecstatic. The Spirit is on him for a day and a night.

Who is a prophet? Who can speak for God? I don't quite know how to answer that one. Once, *Saul* was a prophet. *Saul* the jealous, the greedy, the mad for power. *Saul* the abuser, tormented by demons, the tyrant. *Saul* the oppressor, the one who even on his throne kept a spear in his hand. *He* became a prophet.

Saul's anointing didn't last of course, and his ecstasy wasn't on the same level as an appointed prophet like Jeremiah or Jonah. No, it didn't last more than twenty-four hours.

But it happened.

The role of a prophet is not primarily to tell the future. Nor is it simply to "speak for God" in a vague, ephemeral sort of manner that does not have any clear, underlying aim. Prophecy exists with an edge as keen as Saul's spear—it is a speaking for God against the false powers of the world. Prophecy is a revolutionary act, an act of re-creative dissent, the dissent of God himself against anything in the world—political, economic, systemic, personal—that raises its head against the Lord of love.

This is why Christians use the word *prophetic* to speak of people like Dr. Martin Luther King Jr., Bishop Oscar Romero, Mother Teresa, and many others whose words and lives point to a truth stronger than the vicious systems of human power that are so contrary to the kingdom of God. Their prophecy is forceful and unforgettable precisely to the degree that it lays bare the ever-beating heart of evil that pulsates in the breasts of humans.

Prophecy is the Spirit of creation and creativity using the mouths of men and women to lock the system's joints and bend the world backward, to remember the original goodness and belovedness of what he has made.

Speaking by the Spirit of all love and dissent, the prophets point to what George Eldon Ladd famously termed "the already and the not yet." Generation after generation, the Spirit upends the world, making and unmaking and remaking and brooding over the face of the deep. From every place of absence, he calls out the promise of presence. From every emptiness, form. From every Saul, the simple truths that truly rule the world. False power is overcome by the true.

The Spirit, that holy maker and remaker of the cosmos, speaks an eternal *no* to those who would sop up power to make the world their way. That speaking of the Spirit is carried through the weakness of the prophets into the world, where the spark becomes a fire, igniting all that it brushes.

Saul, scrambling to keep what was never his, is willing to slay innocents, murder family, desecrate holy ground to keep the crown on his brow. And so, as his list of murder attempts lengthens, he pushes and pushes until, with a single breath, the Spirit lays him low who would be high, strips him naked who would wear a crown, and puts him in the dirt who would force others to bow.

PROPHECY IS A REVOLUTIONARY ACT.

We are not told the words Saul uttered. We do not need to know them. Saul's very existence becomes a prophecy. He lies naked in the dust at Samuel's feet, nestled closer to the Spirit of God than he has ever been.

The great irony of Saul's reign is that his most intimate moment with God came apparently against his will, undoing everything he thought he was. But how potent and playful is God's Spirit—that even makes the tyrant revolt against his own reign!

The Spirit, ever playful, ever deadly serious, speaks through Saul, in spite of Saul, against Saul. Saul among the prophets shows the utter failure of worldly power in the face of the mighty weakness of God. It shows how empty the power of kings and emperors is when faced with the simple speakings of the Spirit.

There before Samuel, wicked, paranoid Saul became a prophet who wore a crown no longer his. He breathed revolution against himself.

He was put down, a false prince in the desert, wandering a trackless waste, so close to the very wells of life and wisdom, even pouring them out from his throat, but failing to drink health for his own soul.

Whatever form the gift of prophecy takes in our generation or any other, its outcomes will be the same. Prophets will always speak the Spirit of God's truth in fierce love for the restoration of God's system of power in the face of the whole world's tyranny, violence, and folly.

I walk to the woodshed in the January rain. My flashlight shows the stacked cords resting in even rows. I fill my tub, the last piece cast on top a hunk of knotty fir, all bumps and bends.

I carry the tub to the round block by the porch, fetch the maul, and split the logs one at a time. Good wood, seasoned a couple of years, they crack under the touch of iron. Soon there is only one log left, the malformed one, a challenge to even rest on the block. I do not expect it to split. But I am stubborn and bring the wedge down and down again.

AM I THE KIND OF MAN WHO WOULD BUILD A KINGDOM FOR HIMSELF IN THE DESERT?

Seven times I strike it, with only slivers shaved off from among the knots, until it's hacked about, small enough to be pushed into the firebox. It goes back into the bin, then into the house, then into the stove. For all its resisting, it burns hotter than all the others when I lay fire against it. It pops and mutters as the knots sizzle.

It lies there and burns like a little star, warming my hands. I think of the many people I have dismissed in my life, the many people I have walked past, snubbed, ignored, left unseen. If the Spirit speaks against worldly power, where has he spoken against me? In my search, unconscious though it may have been, for influence, for significance, for the ability to do what I wish, have I set myself up as a miniature Saul?

If I were given the opportunity, am I the kind of man who would build a kingdom for himself in the desert and veneer the murderous mess with God-talk?

I would like to think that I am the humble prophet.

But I wonder if I am the prideful, insecure king.

The flame sputters on.

In *The Stand*, one of Stephen King's characters says, "God don't lay on no bribes, child. He just makes a sign and lets people take it as they will."[3] The Spirit speaks in many ways and in infinite places. He gives both clear teachings and mysteries, words laid as plain as the writings of Paul or Peter and signs as obscure as Saul writhing naked in the desert.

Often we want God to bribe us, though. We ask for him to pay us off somehow, to make a transaction so clear that there is no pondering to be done, no doubt to push through, no power to overthrow.

Sometimes, of course, we feel that we have gotten it. Sometimes he makes signs so clear that there is only room for faith. He allows for confidence, for joyful shouts of the truth, for certainties of the soul. Praise him for it!

But for all the fire that he gives to us at night, he brings clouds sometimes to our day—hiding himself, obscuring the before and the behind. The cloud, the raven, is a sign no less surely than the fire, the dove. For both, he allows us to "take them as we will," correctly or incorrectly. He honors the trails we choose; even if they sometimes lead into folly, he lets us walk them.

Both the clear and the obscure can be the voice of God, the language interpreted and the language hidden.

To the degree that I align with the systems of earthly power, whether through gender, race, wealth, age, vocation, popularity, or success, I must mistrust myself. The Spirit's power of prophecy may intersect worldly systems (King David himself was a prophet), but it will *never* be coextensive with it, and the message of such prophecy will not confirm systems of oppression, exploitation, or pride. The Spirit blows where he will and always moves with love for his creation.

All of his creation.

I must choose. How will I take the clouded signs of God—the prophets like Saul, the crooked trails of deserted Rajneeshpuram? Will I be wise and humble to mark their meaning? Where I am meant to be comforted by their fearsome poetry, will I take comfort? Where I am meant to be challenged by their rough edges, will I rise to meet them?

Will I let both the cloud and fire lead me?

Will you?

In the Bible, in history, and in our present day, true prophets of God are always countermeasures to worldly power. Their rebukes, their mad ramblings, even their validations and encouragements all serve to reorient those in power to the true nature of reality—that God is King, and his reign does not align with accepted political priorities. But as much as we want to make this be about them—about the kings and emperors, the CEOs and legislators, the corporate lawyers killing justice for profit, the untouchable ones who exploit those they are to serve—the truth that lays them low will rarely spare any of us.

We naturally desire to be prophets. But it is also in our nature to cover our ears when we meet true prophets, to tar and feather them, to run them on a rail, to stone, to burn, to crucify them. From the blood of righteous Abel all the way to Zechariah, we love the idea but hate to see our own agenda laid naked in the dust before the Spirit who sees all things clearly.

Are we willing to be changed? Are we willing to give whatever throne we think we own to God's anointed, Jesus? Because it is his reign, in a thousand ways, that the Spirit speaks of, that the Spirit calls us to. And those who exalt themselves before him will surely be humbled. Are you and I ready for every mountain to be laid low, every valley to be raised up? Are we crooked things ready to be made straight? It sounds so good until the hand of God is on our limbs and we know that to set the break our very bones must be snapped and rehealed.

WIND WITH A BODY IS BREATH. BREATH WITH A BODY IS SPEECH. SPEECH WITH THE SPIRIT IS PROPHECY.

Over the face of the deep, the Spirit of creation once brooded. Now, in a world that seeks at every turn to disown its Maker, to upend his good ordering and exchange it for the gruesome power of human corruption, that Spirit of creation is content for a time to whisper. As his power fills the hands of makers like Bezalel with the tools and inspiration to hammer echoes of the coming re-creation into the present reality, so he ignites a fire in the bones of women and men who have been given words to speak. The prophets. Them, us; you, me—if we'll allow the truth in.

Sometimes even if we won't.

And all the weight of Scripture, all the peaceful fire the Spirit has whispered since the canon closed, all the windy prayers, all the groanings that can and cannot be uttered by the church, all the rousing speeches and laments of mourners, all of our words may at times be found to be prophecies. Wherever God's words are spoken and the world is reminded of who is the true and good King of all, there is prophecy; and wherever we allow the truth of Christ, the anointed King, to overcome us, there we become prophets, seers, or spokespeople, Spirit-filled.

Wind with a body is breath. Breath with a body is speech. Speech with the Spirit is prophecy. May we each join our words to that great speech, and may we not force God to peel us naked in the dust.

There is a wind that ever troubles the desert branches, even when no ear hears it.

There is a wind that troubles me with the truth.

THE VOICE OF THE MOUNTAIN

Waiting for the Spirit Who Meets Us

The secret is an open one which the wayfaring man may read. It is simply the old and ever-new counsel: Acquaint thyself with God.
—A. W. Tozer, *The Knowledge of the Holy*

Lost in the cloud, a voice:
Have no fear! We draw near!
Lost in the cloud, a sign:
Son of man! Turn your ear!
—Sufjan Stevens, "The Transfiguration"

Elijah … wrapped his face in his mantle and went out and stood at the entrance of the cave. Then there came a voice to him that said, "What are you doing here, Elijah?"
—1 Kings 19:13

I was wedged into a diagonal basalt crack, barely wider than my body, on an unnamed rock face somewhere near the Eagle Creek trail in northern Oregon. We'd moved off trail and cross country for a while to get here, my two buddies and I having spotted the tempting gray rock face from a spot near Tunnel Falls.

At the base, the ascent had seemed like a good idea. A short chimney climb opened into a large notched crack that curved up to the right, steady and even, high out of sight. One of the three of us didn't feel up to it, so he held our packs while Seth and I stretched. We began the climb.

The chimney was no trouble—a few comfortable surprises of bucket holds and ledges to get our thick boots onto. Then the dicey transition to the crack. That took confidence more than anything, and being less experienced on rock than my friend, I took my cues from one tricky hand-over-hand and made it without incident. Then the long and "easy" part, pressing ourselves upward in a serpentine manner through the V-shaped gouge in the ancient stone, out of sight of the way back down.

And there, about halfway up—long after I had committed my life to the success of this climb—the first voice of wisdom hit me.

What are you doing here?

You, a husband, brother, and son, are risking your life on a climb you are not prepared for, without protection, on a rock face both unknown and unpredictable, with no assurance that there is any kind of exit at the top. You are closer to death than to rescue, and a fool. You will be a dead fool if you make a mistake.

What are you doing here?

It was a good question.

I paused and prayed, attempted some nervous conversation with my friend ahead, and climbed. There was no way forward but to climb. Thirty feet or so farther up, I paused. We'd broken largely above the tree line of the slope below, and the view—well, it was worth the work, if not the danger, of being there. The firs were wreathed in mist, swirling intricately with the breeze from the Eagle Creek canyon. The light playing in the mist came, it seemed, from a dozen impossible directions at once, diffused and bent by the moisture in the air. Colors seemed to play in the haze, unnameable colors at the very edge of the visible spectrum, taunting and inviting and knowing without quite being known. The crisp air off the river, the shriek of osprey, the enduring stillness—all was well, all was very good.

I tucked my arms against my chest, canted my back against the stone behind me, and there, tucked into the rock, I met God.

He had been there the whole time, of course, busy with me and infinite things besides me. I thought of the psalm where David longs like a bird for his mountain, of another where he longs for the shelter of God's feathered wing, of the Song of Songs where the Lover speaks achingly of the "clefts of the rock." God the rock, the protection, the shelter made himself known. While I felt the risk and the danger of my position, at that moment, tucked into prehistoric stone colossally more ancient than the footprints of humans in my land, I felt safe. Utterly sheltered. A witness, cradled by stone, to the beauty of God's Spirit that he makes endlessly around us, even in places without human eye to see or human voice to praise him for it. *It is good that you are here*, the Spirit said.

We use the cliché "mountaintop experience" to refer to a moment in life of particular clarity, power, or joy. It's worn, but I love the phrase—and having summited my share of sizable peaks in the Cascades, I know the feeling.

There is nothing like cresting the huge hunched back of a pre-historic volcano at dawn, seeing the vast triangular shadow of the mountain pointing like some compass for the seraphim, to God knows what, spanning miles. The very thinness of the air sharpens something inside you, and you feel alive at ten or twelve thousand feet in a way that is rare at three or four hundred.

The Bible, always beautifully recursive in its storytelling, whips up the power of that feeling. While the physical mountains of Israel and its surrounding wilderness are dwarfed by most peaks around the world (Mount Zion, that jewel of the earth, is about half the size of the hills out my kitchen window), Scripture utilizes its heights to tower symbolically above the whole earth, as God meets man on the crags of Israel.

Three classic stories demonstrate the point: Moses on Sinai to receive the Law, Elijah on Carmel in his fiery showdown with the minions of Baal, and Christ on the Mount of Transfiguration. Each features the prophet ascending a special mountain, witnessed by his community (faithful Israel in the first example; apostate Israel in the second; Christ's disciples, Moses, and Elijah in the third). At the mountaintop? A revelation! Heaven breaks over earth, and God descends to meet the representative of his people.

On Sinai (Exodus 19) the Law is preceded by thunder and lightning, given with fire. A cloud veils God in beauty, then God in fury—the cloud highlights the King of heaven's holy ferocity. The people, called to be a "priestly kingdom" (v. 6), hesitate and shudder at the foot of the mountain, and send Moses up to receive the Law in their place, even though the invitation was for all of them to climb and meet God (v. 13).

On Carmel? In 1 Kings 18, Elijah faces off with the false and exploitative prophets of Baal, the supposed sky-god. In the ensuing contest between divinities (something like a prophetic cage match), Baal is silent, but God answers Elijah from above with his divine fire, the flame impossibly devouring wood and sacrifice sopping three times over with water.

IN THE BIBLE, IF YOU WANT TO MEET WITH GOD, WHERE DO YOU GO? INTO THE WILDERNESS, AND UP.

On the Mount of Transfiguration (Mark 9), Christ is transformed before his three friends and shines radiant and fearsome. The veiling cloud overshadows it all again, and the voice of God speaks from heaven. Moses and Elijah (those quintessential mountain climbers who stand for the Law and the Prophets) join Jesus the God-man, looking openly upon the face of a God who had veiled himself so often before on these same heights. The vision passes, Christ urges the disciples to keep silence, and they descend.

In the Bible, if you want to meet with God, where do you go? Into the wilderness, and *up*. You climb the holy mountains, the places where earth rises and heaven descends. Yes, you climb, knowing from the past what to expect from God—a display. Power, fire, thunderous speech. Stones carved with the language of heaven. Wicked hosts slain. Figures shrouded in the cloud. Holy ground, holy fear, a radiant face. This pattern is well established throughout Scripture.

Except for 1 Kings 19.

First Kings 19 immediately follows the story I just mentioned of Elijah on Mount Carmel. Elijah, descending from a literal (and figurative) mountaintop experience, is brutally chopped down to size. After the victory over the false prophets and their subsequent execution, Elijah receives a death threat from Jezebel, a bad-news queen with none of her husband Ahab's qualms about going prophet hunting. Elijah runs like a rabbit into the wilderness.

Biblical scholar Jerome Walsh calls Elijah's flight "a series of abandonments."[1] The prophet, victorious over the prophets of Baal, flees the concentric circles of his civilization—Elijah leaves the kingdom, he leaves Judah, he leaves settled land, he leaves all human companionship. He goes deep into the wild desert, where he collapses physically, mentally, and emotionally. Exhausted, he lies down under a bush and sleeps. He eats food brought by a heavenly messenger who tries to get the prophet to get up and act, to go, to do, but Elijah, depressed, refuses until the messenger comes a second time with more to eat. He is barely persuaded to move on.

In the strength of that food, Elijah travels for forty days and nights, over two hundred miles to Horeb, the same mountain as Sinai (called by a different name). He climbs it and enters a cave, a cleft in the rock.

A voice comes.

Why are you here?

The question hangs above the prophet in the air.

In Elijah's mind, perhaps, are voices that he dare not utter: *God, are you such a fool to ask this? You heard the queen's threat, All-Hearing One! All-Seeing One, you saw me, left alone out of all your faithful, limp and spent under the broom bush! All-Knowing One, you knew my fear before it even sprang up in me, as I fled the sword, the wrath, the indifference!*

The words that come out are tempered but full of so much: emotion, betrayal, fear. "I have been very zealous for the LORD, the God of hosts; for the Israelites have forsaken your covenant, thrown down your altars, and killed your prophets with the sword. I alone am left, and they are seeking my life, to take it away" (v. 10).

That is why he is there.

God doesn't directly respond. He only gives a simple command: "Go out and stand on the mountain before the LORD, for the LORD is about to pass by" (v. 11).

All heaven breaks loose. Wind, earthquake, fire. There on Horeb, the same ground where God had burned the bush with fire but did not consume it, the same ground where Moses had been given the words of the Law, the same peak that had been veiled in cloud and struck by lightning not entirely natural, the same place where God was accustomed to come in power—in that place, power came.

Walsh's present-tense translation of the Hebrew captures the power of the moment:

> Look! Yahweh is passing by! And a wind, great and
> strong, splits mountains and breaks rocks into pieces
> before Yahweh! But Yahweh is not in the wind. And

after the wind, an earthquake! But Yahweh is not
in the earthquake. And after the earthquake, a fire!
But Yahweh is not in the fire. And after the fire, a
sound of sheer silence![2]

At this meeting of God and man on the mountain, God is not
in the display of power, the expected, the routines of divine-human
interaction. He isn't in the fearful, the awe-bringing, the explosive.
Instead, as the dust fades, as the rubble grumbles into the last fits and
trickles of landslides, as the embers crinkle and fade, something is left
behind them. Left in spite of them. A presence in absence.

"A still, small voice," is the traditional translation; literally in
Hebrew, "the voice of silence, thin."

The thin sound of silence.

The prophet recognizes his master's call in the stillness *after* the
classic display. This time God is not in the flame and racket; he is in
the silence. Cautious in the presence of even the quiet Holy, Elijah
hoods himself with his fur cloak and steps out on the face of the
mountain. He meets God.

All the fireworks and gunpowder—and what does God ask? The
question already whispered in the dark of the cave.

Why are you here?

What was God doing with this foolish show? Why does he ask the
burning question twice—phrased identically in a strange little litany?

Why are you here?

God is reminding Elijah—so enamored yet afraid—of power, of displays of might, of Jezebel's threats, of the fire from heaven that can be seen and heard and felt. God is reminding him that the true power behind the cosmos is as potent and unnerving when invisible and silent as when carried by lightning and thunder. The Spirit, breathing silent as thought, gives the gift of his voice to him, not merely in what is said, but doubly in what is unsaid. This time on Horeb, the display was empty, the emptiness of silence the true display. God was, very simply, in what he chose to be in, not in what anyone would expect from an appearance of God.

God may or may not reveal himself according to our expectations. The ways of the Spirit are strange ways—strange and sometimes silent, but always good.

Behind Elijah's despair at what could be seen—apostate Israel, the death threat of a queen renowned for violence, a parched land reeling with drought—was the hope of what could not be seen. Seven thousand, God tells him, who have not kissed the idol. A path down the mountain and out of the wilderness.

But at times of great pain and stress, times of confusion or brutality, when death has come to one I love, when I have been treated unjustly, when friends are far away, all that I want, all that I feel I could listen to, is the voice on the mountain that comes with power. With seen power. With the fire, the wind, and the earthquake that shatters stone before the Lord.

Perhaps, at such times, that is why God rarely gives it.

How do you know when you are in God's presence? What do you expect to feel when God speaks to you? How do you expect to know his voice? Should you ever hear it on the mountain, would you be brave enough to cover your face and answer the Spirit?

Another voice, another moment. This time the voice comes from the throat of the apostle Paul, and the mountain is Mars Hill, outside of the city-state of Athens. This mountain is impossibly far from Horeb, both in mileage and type—Mars Hill is populated rather than desolate, abuzz with the voices of classic philosophers rather than silent, a place of wisdom and urbane discussion rather than one of mystic revelation. Athens offers a thousand sensible theories for the nature of everything, rather than mystery, the labyrinthine trails of Sinai.

THE WAYS OF THE SPIRIT ARE STRANGE WAYS—STRANGE AND SOMETIMES SILENT, BUT ALWAYS GOOD.

Mars Hill—where the voices on the mountain are those of the Stoics and the Epicureans, the poet-philosophers of Greece, the background chorus the calls to worship for a thousand gods that can be seen, fed, kissed by human lips. Acts 17 reveals a catcalling marketplace of ideas, a panoply of divinities and worldviews.

Paul enters this cacophony of truths and untruths, finding an ancient altar dedicated to an "unknown God." By the invitation of the locals, he preaches. Riffing on the mysterious God of the altar, he quotes Greek poets in support of the gospel. Paul says that it is universally human to

> search for God and perhaps grope for him and find him—though indeed he is not far from each one of us. For "In him we live and move and have our being"; as even some of your own poets have said, "For we too are his offspring."
>
> Since we are God's offspring, we ought not to think that the deity is like gold, or silver, or stone, an image formed by the art and imagination of mortals. While God has overlooked the times of human ignorance, now he commands all people everywhere to repent. (vv. 27–30)

What are we doing here? We all grope for God in whatever way we are predisposed. Along every trail of our lives, we grope for him. The lucky brush him from time to time. The blessed are given faith to sustain them at times when the brushing seems impossible. But however spent in our journey we may be, under broom bush, in cave, or worshipping at our favorite shrine among a thousand pagan altars, God is not far from any one of us. Not far from the persecuted, the depressed. Not far from the Epicurean, who seeks the divine through every pleasure. Not far from the Stoic, who seeks him through denial and asceticism.

The Spirit is near, here. Whether in fire, wind, quake, or the thin voice of silence, he may be found by those who reach out. This closeness is not easy for us (he will ask questions that we do not want to answer), but his presence is *life*, waiting patiently for all who will turn.

Even while we grope, feeling blindly in cave or crevice, the Spirit is not far away. He is *who* we move within, live within—in whom we find our being. The Creator and Sustainer, limitlessly infinite to every one of us, and choosing to reveal himself in love and rough kindness.

The joy of it! But the implication of that infinity and depth and goodness of being is this: however we seek to limit the immortal, we shall fail. Our images of him—physical like the idols of Athens, or abstract like Elijah's notion of God as an abandoner—fall cruelly short. The imaginations of mortals, whether prophet, philosopher, me, or you, fall short. There is no theology that can contain such a one. On the mountain there is only the reaching for a silent voice outside the cave; a trust, perhaps, that the keeper of the voice, even against appearances, is here and is *good*.

Even these words are a conception, an image. I strain for truth and clarity—but I am only groping. If the Spirit was not kind and joyful to reveal, to revel in the knowing and being known by his many offspring, then hope for any of us would be a joke.

But hope is not a joke.

Environmentalist Paul Hawken, in the 2009 commencement address to the University of Portland, said, "Ralph Waldo Emerson once asked what we would do if the stars only came out once every thousand years. No one would sleep that night, of course. The world would create new religions overnight. We would be ecstatic, delirious, made rapturous by the glory of God. Instead, the stars come out every night and we watch television."[3]

God met Elijah in a special way on Horeb. But for us today his presence by his Spirit is no less. In him we live, we move, we have our being. In him the seven stars are out, always out. They burn with the ancient fire from outside, a fire of power, a fire of kindness and beneficence, a fire of pure love.

The infinite Creator often chooses to whisper, even to speak through the nothingness of stillness itself. But oh, the stars are out. Why do we turn up the television?

THE SPIRIT IS NOT FAR AWAY. HE IS WHO WE MOVE WITHIN, LIVE WITHIN— IN WHOM WE FIND OUR BEING.

"It's hard to hear the gentle whisper of the Spirit amid the noise of Christendom,"[4] Christian activist Shane Claiborne said once. It is indeed. This is for many reasons, external and internal. The external are easier to see and probably easier to change. The constant hum of Christian culture (at least in the West) urges and nags us to engage, consume, respond, react, buy.

But to twist Claiborne's quote, it's also hard to hear the gentle whisper of the Spirit amid the noise of *Christians*. Our inner noise. Very few people (I am rarely one of them) are mature enough to be quiet and wise enough to know and accept the Spirit's presence when the world is silent and dark.

Polish nun Maria Faustina Kowalska once wrote, "The Holy Spirit does not speak to a soul that is distracted and garrulous. He speaks by His quiet inspirations to a soul that is recollected, to a soul that knows how to keep silence."⁵ But even this is only a half-truth, an image. It is true, but not *always* true—the voice of the mountain proves that. If we are to learn anything, it must be that *the Spirit speaks the way he chooses.*

There are two kinds of Christians: those who expect God to be the voice from the cloud and those who climb expecting the voice of "thin silence." I have met people whose lives were shaped by divine visions and who claim audible words from the Lord. I am not one to pick holes in another's journey up Sinai. But I also know people who have spent years of listening, having caught (at best) only a bare *Why are you here?* To them the Spirit has spoken in his rich silence, groanings too deep for words. The Spirit reveals himself as he chooses. But he is never far away.

There are two kinds of Christians—no, there are two *more* kinds: those who think they can make God do something and those who know they cannot. Distrust those who claim they can climb the mountain anytime they choose and come back with a word from God.

The Spirit is faithful, but he will not come running when we whistle for him. He is kind but will not jump for us. He may give a show, but when he speaks, it will be in his good way for his good reasons. And who can tell him either to speak or to keep silent? We can only ask and trust.

We must cast down our images of God, smash and open our imaginations, search the Scriptures and listen for the sometimes-silent voice. We must ask the Spirit to speak, to reveal, to be known in *his* way, in *his* time. We must know and be known. This gift, this knowing, is the voice of the mountain. It shines stubbornly from God's love to humble us—to blind the proud and give light to the meek. It shines so that in the Spirit's way and the Spirit's time, our faces might shine with the revelations of the mountain.

He brings down the haughty, you know, even when the haughty are his own, and he raises those who are low. His power can look like weakness, and his weakness is limitless strength.

So we cast down our idols, even the ones that look like God. We turn ever to the old truths, to the Word, to the sacraments, to a journey of good abandonments, the inward journey. The ascent of the mountain is our business. Attention is our business. The speaking? Well, that is the Spirit's business, and who can say how his voice will come to any one of us?

WE MUST ASK THE SPIRIT TO SPEAK, TO REVEAL, TO BE KNOWN IN HIS WAY, IN HIS TIME.

What can be known is that his words will be ones in keeping with his character—breathing life, making love bloom where there was no love, restoring justice, and remaking what is bent or broken.

The Spirit's voice—always, without exception—will bring the fruit of the Spirit that Paul lists in the letter to the Galatians: *love, joy, peace, patience, kindness, generosity, faithfulness, gentleness,* and *self-control.* Against such things there is no law, on Sinai or in any valley. And so, whether the voice on the mountain burns like fire in the clouds, blisters us like the wind of the wilderness, rattles us like the quake of holy ground, or simply … whispers, it will speak. It will ask us questions that we do not want to answer, send us places we do not want to go, and remind us that the great goodness of a God of mountains is that however far our ascent to meet him may feel, his descent of love to meet us is infinitely greater.

Why are you here? hangs in the air, but even in the same breath the old love is felt: *It's good that you are; how wonderful that you exist!*

So we climb. Climb and listen. The high places are the Spirit's, shimmering with color, lively with fire and wind, but with the fire-voice, the whisper-voice, the thin-silence-voice muttering love where we do not expect it. This is his way. It is good.

At times in life, we must run into the desert. We go through our own abandonments—of routine, of community, of faith in anything seen or unseen, perhaps even of a hope for such faith. We throw ourselves down, spent, discouraged, depressed; silent outside, screaming within.

The voice on the mountain is there for us. Like Job's friends who sat and mourned for seven days without saying a word, God's thin voice of sheer silence can be present when words are too much. We all climb that mountain in our lives. And however unpredictable his means will be, the outcome of his silence or speech will always and ever be love—the love that called us up; the love in which we live and move and have our being; the love of God, the first and deepest Lover.

We don't often call such difficult times "mountaintop experiences." Yet that is what they are. We climb to meet God, to commune with his Spirit. That Spirit knows when to speak through a voice and when to speak through silence. And in the shimmering colors at the edge of our peripheral vision, turning gray and aquamarine, and sandy brown and brilliant fire red, he glitters. In the ringing of the ears after the gun goes off, after the rockslide, after the heaving ground, he speaks. By whatever means he chooses, for whatever needs we have.

He calls us. He meets us. *Why are you here?* he asks, though he knows that and every other answer. He is patient, good, kind, ferocious. He breaks rocks to let us hear the silence after they split. The Spirit who takes us up the mountain will be faithful to lead us down.

Perhaps some who ascend in the dark will descend in the light.

The mist rose and writhed. The gray firs steamed where the sun began to break through and touch them. I tried to memorize it all at once—the smell of the air, the cool of the stone at my back, the view, the feelings (mixed like water and oil) of fear and wellness that were with me on the rock face.

I tried to know the stillness I found there, and to let it know me. And I continued my climb. The crack continued to curve gently up the face. It seemed made for climbers, a basalt slide in reverse that opened up to deposit us gently at the top of the ridge. We followed a game trail down to a stream, the stream down to the scree field of the rock face. We laughed an awful lot at the foot, great yips and howls that echoed in the woods.

Then we were back on the trail.

I was quiet on our hike back, but it was a strong quiet, strong and good.

FROM THE STUMP OF JESSE
Welcoming the Spirit of Messiah

Hey dove
who delivered salvation,
who is like as you are?
—Wovenhand, "Coup Stick"

Christ stood over sickness of a cruel kind ...
all weeds now must spring up as herbs,
the seas slip apart.
—"The Lay of the Nine Herbs" (traditional Saxon)

A shoot shall come out from the stump of Jesse,
and a branch shall grow out of his roots.
The spirit of the LORD shall rest on him,
the spirit of wisdom and understanding,
the spirit of counsel and might,
the spirit of knowledge and the fear of the LORD.
—Isaiah 11:1–2

It's a dryish day in January. I walk past wide-ringed stumps into the forest, gathering branches for kindling our woodstove.

Green wood doesn't burn well. Nor do branches that have lain on the forest floor too long. But there is a point—after the moisture from inside has left, and before the moisture from outside has entered—when the fallen branch lying in the loam is *perfect*. It can look wet, rotten in the bark even. It can seem the most unburnable bit of brush in the world. But if you know what you are looking for, you will pick it up. You'll snap it or score it with a hatchet. Even in the dead wet of winter, you will see and smell that it's dry and ready.

In the 1990s a great fire swept down over the ridge behind our woods. Twenty-odd years later, the standing stumps and snags are still blackened, gritting off into charcoal when you scrape them with a finger. The dead limbs and trunks have a sterile fullness, their abundant skeletons marking the line of the old fire, which the locals say burned for three days and three nights, maybe more, maybe less. Time compressed while the woods burned, leaving this ragged border where the fire cleansed the heights of trees, where the blackened clefts of rock are still exposed.

How strange are the borders of all natural places! The edges, the ridges, the boundary lines unspoken but marked as if by a spell. How strange are the beaches, the riverbanks, the dry creek beds. How strange are the tree lines, the cliffs, the borderlines where the wind hits heavy. The here-and-theres, the hello and good-bye places, the spots of opening and closing, binding and loosing. The meetings of air and earth, of water and fire, of man and God.

How strange are the places of stumps! How very good.

For such strangeness, I have noticed, is the most fertile soil for sprouts.

To understand the secret of the stump, we must understand one of the most important stories in the Old Testament—that of David, the shepherd king. David was not Israel's first king (that dubious honor belongs to Saul, and we've seen how he wore the crown), but he was the nation's most important one.

Why "the stump of Jesse" and not of "David"? A Hebrew turn of a phrase for one, and a reminder of the moment (in David's father Jesse's household) 1 Samuel 16 tells us about, when the Spirit of the Lord first came on David in power. God speaks to the prophet Samuel, instructing him to leave his grief over the failure of Saul as king, and go seek out a certain Jesse, from Bethlehem, to anoint a new king from among his sons. Jesse makes seven of his sons pass before the prophet. Samuel is eager to anoint the good-looking older boys, but the Lord stays his hand. Samuel politely asks if any sons have been forgotten. Of course—they've overlooked the baby of the family. Someone tromps off through the tall grass to fetch David, who'd been forgotten out in the sheep fields.

Samuel sees the little shepherd. Then the whole world comes together.

> The LORD said, "Rise and anoint him; for this is the one." Then Samuel took the horn of oil, and anointed him in the presence of his brothers; and the spirit of the LORD came mightily upon David from that day forward. (vv. 12–13)

Isaiah's words are the repetition of an origin story, a replanting, if you will. It was in the house of Jesse that so many beginnings began, and to that place the story of another unexpected anointed one, the Messiah, must return.

Many years later, after Goliath and caves and wars and coups and wives and palaces, the shepherd boy, now the king of his anointing, is given a vision of the great things that were held in the prophet's horn of oil. God, speaking through the prophet Nathan in 2 Samuel 7, said to David,

> I took you from the pasture, from following the sheep to be prince over my people Israel; and I have been with you wherever you went, and have cut off all your enemies from before you; and I will make for you a great name, like the name of the great ones of the earth.... Moreover the LORD declares to you that the LORD will make you a house. When your days are fulfilled and you lie down with your ancestors, I will raise up your offspring after you, who shall come forth from your body, and I will establish his kingdom. He shall build a house for my name, and I will establish the throne of his kingdom forever. I will be a father to him, and he shall be a son to me.... Your house and your kingdom shall be made sure forever before me; your throne shall be established forever. (vv. 8–9, 11–14, 16)

If you see Jesus here, it's because he is. Whatever reference to David's immediate kids and grandkids, the promise of God to build a house through David's line, the house built by the ruler of an eternal kingdom, a "forever" kingdom, is the promise of the true Anointed King, of whom David is a backward echo, a sound heard before the trumpet blast itself.

God promised that David's line would be a lineage of power, goodness, and deliverance. True rulership, good rulership. God promised that David's family would be the house builders of an eternal kingdom.

That promise—to all appearances—didn't even last as long as David did. Being a "man after God's own heart" notwithstanding, David's kingly track record included vast bloodshed—so much killing, in fact, that God didn't want him to build a temple. It included the randy affair with Bathsheba and the murder of her husband, Uriah, and the little matter of an arrogant census against good counsel that brought deadly pestilence on the land. While David had his strong points, he was not the Anointed King for whom the land longed.

But still, the line of the shepherd-king, the poet and prophet from Bethlehem (as his distant grandchild Jesus would be), offered hope as the reign of David faded and a successor, Solomon, was named. David's son led the little kingdom of Israel into a golden age of wisdom and wealth, and all seemed well, until you scratched the surface. Under a veneer of intellectual wisdom, Solomon's discretion and righteousness was horrifically stunted. He was power hungry, amassing riches and exotic weaponry against the express command of God. He was lustful, and indulgent of idol-worshipping spouses, and for all the moves he makes toward building God a temple, it is a far cry from the "house" that the Spirit promised through the prophet that David's eternal kingdom would bring.

It's after Solomon, though, that things get truly nasty. The line of David, decadent and decayed within a few short generations, cannot even hold the kingdom of Israel together. The country divides in a civil war, the twin kingdoms of the north and south vacillating between the worship of the old gods of the land (so dark and blood hungry that some biblical writers cannot bring themselves to write their proper names) and tepid repentances and turnings back to the God who led their people out of slavery and into a land of promise.

GOD'S SPIRIT IS A CONSTANT REVEALER OF HIMSELF, OF THE FATHER, OF THE SON.

How quickly David's tree fell! And at the time Isaiah was written, some ten generations after David, of the thousand images of fallen glory that could have been selected, "stump" was chosen, the "stump of Jesse," the stump not only of the royal family of Israel and Judah but the stump of hope itself—the hope of a righteous ruler, of power in the hands of a worthy one rather than a line of bloody or cowering tyrants. The stump of goodness, strength, and wonder. The stump of God's promise that all the earth should be blessed by the children of Abraham, the descendants of lionlike Judah.

The "stump of Jesse." It seems a cruel way to describe a royal family. I'm not sure what to compare it to for my American people— maybe the "bones of the Roosevelts" or the "husk of the Kennedys." Picture a family that symbolizes power, rulership. A dynasty, rich and potent. Now sour and wither the image, kill it, for all appearances. If that image is a tree, fruitful, mighty, and promising, chop it down. Lay the ax at its very roots and fell the sucker.

A tree, you see, once grew here in the house of the kings, a tree transplanted from the sheep fields, from Bethlehem. But it is gone, and Jesse is the root you have to dig to hit the green in the dead wood again. For the author of Isaiah, the banded stump, inner rings laid bare for the counting, is the image of the kings of the line of David. The line of promise is dead.

But the stump, on all these strange borderlands of history and brutality, disappointment and hope, somehow holds hope. The prophet sees some inner life. The bark is dead. The pith of the wood is green yet.

The prophet says that it shall sprout.

God's Spirit is a constant revealer of himself, of the Father, of the Son.

That revelation has come in many ways. One is through "general" revelation, which is given by God to all peoples at all times and places in history. Paul's famous opening arguments in Romans, certain psalms, and many ancient and beautiful myths ("good dreams," C. S. Lewis called them[1]) that persist in folk cultures around the globe, stories suspiciously similar to the Christ story, are examples.

"Special" revelation refers to the kind of knowledge-giving that the Spirit employed to speak with direct and unusual clarity to particular peoples throughout history. Every time we read, "And the word of the LORD came," in Scripture, we catch the quickened heart of special revelation. Christians believe that we experience this special revelation uniquely in the Bible—inspired by the Spirit (who "carried along" holy writers, Peter said [2 Peter 1:21 ESV]) to be a Book of books, flawed in the ways that books are flawed, perfect in a way that no other book is, as full of the cloud and fire of the Spirit's hiddenness and revelation as the wilderness was while Israel wandered in it.

This revelation extends past the closing of the biblical canon and through every generation of the church. The Spirit is today's special revelator, offering insight, wisdom, and discernment. He balances the words of life found in the Bible with the fire that burns in us and, if invited to work, sets us ablaze in a fire of life.

We could talk about the revealing work of the Spirit for longer than a lifetime, but there is a pinnacle to it: the Word made flesh, Jesus of Nazareth, the anointed Christ.

The Messiah.

Today, living over two thousand years after the closing of the Bible's canon, we find it easy to backread two millennia of Christian theology into the Bible—particularly older sections of the Bible such as Isaiah. We forget that some things made clear to us after Christ's ascension and the founding of the church seem to have been mysteries in the ages that preceded us.

We walk, as it were, backward through time, carrying with us the interpretations of a popular TV pastor, our mother, our barber, our favorite theologian. We wander back through the centuries, across the gritty lands of the Bible, and like tourists stepping out of a rented time machine, lightly sit down by the ancient words of the prophets.

We have Polaroids in hand, ready to capture a devotional snapshot, often heedless of the context we've landed in.

When this promise of the sprouting stump was penned, it represented the bleeding edge of God's work in the world. We've already seen that the kingship of the Davidic line was a bitter disappointment when compared to the promise that God made toward the family of the simple shepherd from Bethlehem. The ancient hopes that God would reach into history and save his people, that the serpent's head would be ground into the dust, that Abraham's seed would scatter like swimming stars, that David would never lack a righteous son to sit on the throne—those hopes were spent. The tree had been felled, and the stump sat, its sap cowering down in the deep roots.

THE PROMISE OF THE SPROUT FEELS DISTANT SOMETIMES, BUT IT IS THE PROMISE THAT MY OWN BROKENNESS IS BEING CONSUMED IN LIFE FROM OUTSIDE ME.

But wait, said Isaiah, there's something stirring. Of the stump, theologian Walter Brueggemann wrote, "Now, in the face of that spent hope, the poet asserts a new generativity with a sprout, unnamed and unidentified, but a faint sign of life, growth, and possibility ... the coming of a royal figure in time to come who will positively enact all that is best in royal power, all that the Davidic kings heretofore had failed to accomplish."[2]

The poet sees a sprout! Green in the dead wood! And why?

Brueggemann said, "The explanation offered for this inexplicable coming reality is 'the spirit of the Lord.' … Yahweh's generative, irresistible, authorizing 'wind' upon David … a force that enlivens, gives power, energy, and courage, so that its bearer is one designated, who has the capacity to do what the world believes is impossible."[3]

The stump of Jesse sprouts under the wind of God—the Spirit. And with the curl of the impossible sprout comes the hope of good impossibilities.

Including you. Including me.

This is the hope I feel when my heart falls speechless at the brutality of wicked rulers, corporate oligarchs, corrupt politicians, and far-off warlords and ethnic cleansers—every one of whose victims was made, like me, in the beloved image of the beloved God. The promise of the sprout feels distant sometimes, but it is the promise that my own brokenness is being consumed in life from outside me, that my own broken borders of mind, soul, and body hold hope of green life. The hope that my sin may be redeemed, that my failings will be bound up, that my broken bones will be set, that my every disappointment will find a single radiant hope, weak and green. Inviolable. Inexorable.

Like the Spirit upon him.

The first plant that I taught my children to recognize was the humble lawn plantain. Those of you from more tropical places think "short banana" when I say plantain, but for me, the word means a lowly green sprout, a wayside plant that loves the soft trailing places where feet and hooves and tires go.

I learned as a boy that its leaves are better than bandages. It is a gentle astringent, drawing and closing cuts, stings, and scratches, accelerating healing like something out of a fairy tale. It's edible too (medieval pilgrims called it "way-bread"), but if you try it (after triple-checking your identification), eat only the bright young shoots. The older leaves are only good for stews and bandages.

Plantain grows only in disturbed places. You will see it bordering trails and gravel driveways, along old country roads, in gullies and drainage ditches, in fields turned over and forgotten, and along footpaths trod one time too few to keep the new growth down.

For a wound, you pluck a few leaves, wash them in clean water, and nibble them with your front teeth. No need to chew, just a couple dozen little nips to break the leaves and mix your saliva into the juices of the leaves. Then you press the mashed leaves gently on the wound. If you are treating a child, tell a story, such as that the fairies taught you this remedy. If you are treating an adult, reassure your patient that the poultice is not poison.

Let the healing sprout work.

Jesus said that for a man to gain his life, he must lose it. He said that the kingdom of heaven is like the smallest seed you've ever heard of—look now and you can barely see it; wait and it will be big enough for the nesting of every bird. He said the kingdom is like a treasure buried, like a secret pearl, like the found thing that was once lost, and like the lost thing that is more valuable than all the things that are found. He saw the hope of life in every secret thing, in every strange and borderland place, in the overlooked plantain by the pilgrim paths. In the ash-colored snags and scree where fire played, he saw orchards.

Perhaps he saw such hope because he was such a hope.

Isaiah 11 is the place where the "sevenfold" gifts of the Spirit are most clearly expressed. What does the Spirit of the Lord bring to this shoot from Jesse's stump?

First, "the Spirit of the LORD" resting on him. The Spirit of God himself is the first gift, and the following six examine facets of the gift, the qualities that the Spirit brings to the Chosen One. Thus, the remaining six gifts are, in fact, transmittable qualities of the Spirit, gifts given by giving himself. What kind of Spirit is this gift? It (he) is: "The Spirit of wisdom and understanding, the Spirit of counsel and might, the Spirit of knowledge and the fear of the LORD" (v. 2, adapted from the NRSV).

Seven, the number of completion, the number of perfections of God's Spirit, means that this passage has been viewed for centuries as the way to think most completely about the ways that God's Spirit rested on his representative, the expected Jewish Messiah, the son of David and true King, Jesus of Nazareth, as hailed in holy foolishness by Christians.

Pause for a moment, and return to the great disappointment of David's line. All the best of David's heritage is here—the wisdom and understanding of Solomon, the might and fear of the God of David. The vision here that the prophet sees may start as a stump, but it includes the promise of a rugged and mighty tree.

The prophet sees a supernaturally gifted king, one of which any people used to monarchy would dream. We humans are so used to tyranny and human systems of power and government that we likely wouldn't even know what a "godly" leader was if one rose up. Still, if we quiet ourselves, we can feel the hope that a good monarch would bring—even for someone like me, the child of an upstart two-century-old republic.

This hope is for a leader arising from a quarter unheard of, a leader who judges with justice, not by appearances. Through some second sight, this leader sees through the way things *seem* to be, to the very pith of them, to the way they *are*, and does something about the truth.

THE SPIRIT RE-CREATES THROUGH THE GIVEN SON, AND CREATION BLOOMS IN PEACE.

This hope is for a righteous leader of our people, an advocate for the poor and oppressed, one who judges fairly for the meek of the earth and whose breath slays the wicked (the sword passes from his lips, as in John's Revelation), displaying the power of the word of the Word to decimate cruelty and oppression, to cut off all wickedness.

It is as if the strong and thickening shoot is wrapped in righteous faithfulness, wrapped with it like the heavy belt of a warrior-king. And the result? Creation itself is beautifully subverted, remade. The gift that the Lord's Spirit brings flowers infinitely, changes the very ecology of the earth. It reconciles predator and prey, the powerful and the vulnerable, diverting the channels of life into the dry and long-forgotten creek bed of peace.

The Spirit re-creates through the given Son, and creation blooms in peace. In the knowledge of the Spirit, the ancient flood arises once more to heal, but this time to heal through gentle life, not through death and drowning. The knowledge of God covers the earth like waters cover the sea. The Spirit of God once more broods in flourishing and love and kind creation over the face of the deep.

How blessed are the borders, strange and bare and rich, of every natural place. How blessed are the cuttings, the ash heaps, the places of the stump. I say more: how blessed is Christ, the green sprout of Jesse, the upstart of creation. We were a stump, our whole fallen race, and by God's Spirit he has become our first green sign of hope. We did not look for him, but he bloomed anyway, and the world blossoms in his footprints.

This is a primal mystery of union. Jesus, the Word made human flesh, was the promised sprout of the stump because the Spirit of the Lord was on him, filling him. That same Spirit of gifting is on us, filling us.

When, midway through his ministry in Judea, Jesus sent his followers out to preach and heal, he pulled them close to him and, in a sacramental moment, *breathed* on them. This act signified that he was passing his Spirit to them, signifying the life-breath of the Creator and Re-creator going into the sprout of a new humanity.

It was a gift and a blessing specially given for the special work that he'd asked them to do, a forecast of greater things to come.

HOW BLESSED IS CHRIST, THE GREEN SPROUT OF JESSE, THE UPSTART OF CREATION.

That breath of giving was the sprout from the stump of Jesse branching out to bear fruit after his kind. Where the king of the ancient line had healed, now he called his friends, his siblings to heal. What the Son of David had preached, he empowered them to preach.

They were to go out as emissaries of the King, *as emissaries that bore the same power of kingship that was on their leader.* They bore, through the breath, the Spirit, power to bind and loose, to work with authority, to bless and to shake the dust of the apostate off of their feet.

"Greater works you will do than those you've seen me do," he said of those who believe in him (John 14:12, my paraphrase). Why? Because they, filled with the Spirit of good kingship, of truth and healing, have the power to do so in his name, the name of the heir of a strange and unseen throne, carrying the King's seal to make visible an eternal kingdom that has no borders and yet is ever a place of boundaries.

Here is a beauty and a wonder: in his patience and wisdom, God—Father, Son, and Spirit—has chosen to be one who waits to remake and renew. The maker of all, who has made all makers, breathes the Spirit on us through the lips of his Son (made like us). And so, like the Seventy, we are sent.

To where? To what work? To everywhere. To all works. To the disturbed places, the marked places, the borderlands where plantain grows and waits to heal, and is overlooked because its power is not recognized.

The gift of the Spirit remains, the breath on the forehead, the anointing of wind. It kisses and winnows, remaking us makers into remakers. Into those who would bring the kingdom as the King is, in any way that we are able. To code computers and farm, to teach and baptize, to plant plantain and pluck it and press it to the blood of the wounds. In humility to press it to our own wounds, recognizing that we are part of the creation being healed day by day, the creation that yet groans for an upheaval, for the King's full reign.

To redeem the borders where the wind hits heavy, to mark them all in the healing power of the way-bread.

Strange trails are good places to bloom.

The stump of Jesse sprouted. And if you can believe it, the wisp of green that crept up from the rings of a dead dynasty in Palestine has thickened, bloomed, and is even now fruiting. It is a tree, a vine, a mighty shading plant on a hill, and all those born of the Spirit are becoming its branches.

This is the green of hope out of the dead ground, a fresh and lively shoot of life from ash and rot and sickness of earth.

It is, as poet David Rosenberg wrote, inspired by a different passage of Isaiah,

> *as if the heart of the world's body*
> *were on a line*
> *descended from David.*[4]

Indeed! Watch for a moment the green life of Jesus, the Spirit-gifted sprout life of Jesus. That heart of all of us flashes between moments, sprouting under a strange star from the east, shooting up in wisdom and stature and favor, learning, teaching, wandering, healing, hurting, weeping, shouting, convicting, convicted, hung on a tree and pierced until his water ran out as if pressed from green grain, planted again (like a heart that is a seed, or a grain of wheat that falls) in the ground, into the ever-present abyss, into death, into a borrowed tomb, a cleft in the rock.

From which darkness, by the power of the Spirit, the dead heart's rings split, shuddered, and sent up a second sprout of green. Give it just a little while—his branches will hold up every bird that wishes for a place to rest, and we will all, every tongue, tribe, and nation, sing of the stump of Jesse, which was dead, but—*behold!*—lives.

Oh, what a tree that heart has become.

His roots run deeper than the world.

THE RENEWER OF EARTH
Honoring the Spirit Who Sustains

The Holy Ghost is the substantial vigour of all creatures
whatsoever. Every creature has a beam of God's glory in it.
—*The Works of Richard Sibbes*, vol. IV

There lives the dearest freshness deep down things …
Because the Holy Ghost over the bent
World broods with warm breast and with ah! bright wings.
—Gerard Manley Hopkins, "God's Grandeur"

When you send forth your spirit, they are created;
and you renew the face of the ground.
—Psalm 104:30

A few factors make up a guitar's "tone," an instrument's unique voice. The quality, species, and resonance of the wood of the body, the shape of construction and bracing, the finish, the material and tension of the strings all affect the sound produced. But every guitar, and indeed all stringed instruments, also must possess the quality of "sustain," the ability to hold the sound of a note once the string is set vibrating. The pleasure and expression of the instrument, its ability to put a musician's feelings into notes, is in great part due to sustain. From ukulele to piano, samisen to dulcimer, harp to harpsichord, banjo to violin—they all behave this way. Who, after all, would care for music that had no duration?

A note is plucked. Tuned to vibrate at a particular frequency, the string oscillates in an undulating wave, rising and falling like a swell of the water, its constituent frequency attended by many smaller competing harmonics, but with the overwhelming force of one in *particular*—the note the player wished to strike.

Pluck.

The string is set in motion, heaving, shaking, like a thing alive.

Music begins!

But all things have a life span, from the note of a lute to an orchestral arrangement. Nothing lasts forever (or so it first appears), and the same principles of decay that govern bodies and plants and planets hold sway in music too. A brief millisecond passes after the initial release of the string, and already the ringing note is decreasing in volume, degrading evenly (if left untouched) until it quiets, loses clarity, becomes imperceptible to the human ear, and then (long after we've ceased to hear it) stops moving. It returns to its rest, to stasis, kinetic energy once again only potential, waiting for the next will of the musician.

Of course, most musicians place many, many notes in a row, differing in pitch, duration, and volume, and often many all at one time, producing beautiful things that we call melody and harmony, beat, chords and glissandos, symphonies and lullabies, folk songs and punk songs, and more.

Sustain, for as long as the musician wills the notes to last.

One of the most beautiful works of the Holy Spirit (whom Abraham Kuyper called "the one omnipotent Worker of all life and quickening"[1]) is the sustaining of the world. Yes, he made all things, but both the Old and New Testaments clearly (and lushly) teach that he sustains all things too.

HE HOLDS UP ALL OF CREATION, KEEPS ALL NATURE LIKE SO MANY PLUCKED NOTES IN A UNIVERSAL SYMPHONY.

In the same love with which the Spirit bent and brooded happily over the unformed waters, in the same love with which he spoke all things into being in harmony with the Word and the Father, he sustains all things. This is the constant providence of God's Spirit. He holds up all of creation, keeps all nature like so many plucked notes in a universal symphony, according to the laws he has made. Inexpressibly complex music are we all, yet brilliantly simple.

Think of it. At no moment from our conception until now has the Holy Spirit's ceaseless sustaining work failed to hold our inmost molecules in order. He is with us, with everything, the Weaver of all of reality, as present at every point of the warp and woof of creation as at every other, strumming the loom, shuttling the threads into place.

Mathematically, all points can be considered the center of an infinite plane, and by this all places may be called the Spirit's home. He is as present with us this moment, keeping the nuclei of our inner atoms revolving, as he is in the farthest nebulae, in the most untouched crevasse of a glacier unexplored by human feet, in the fire and magma of the earth's deep core. Sustaining, watching. In his own way, sanctifying all things according to their nature. Being. Making be. Loving. Being beloved.

But somehow I numb to the wonder. I forget that every action I take in this rich and multiform creation affects countless other precious notes in the symphony of God. I forget that the Spirit views my treatment of all he calls "very good" as extensions of my heart toward himself. My thoughtless casting of a reusable resource in the trash, my barely touched heart on hearing of human or ecological disaster and suffering.

I am not alone in my forgetting. We Christians forget the closeness that the Creator of all things keeps with his creation. In our overwhelming emphasis on God's transcendence (a rich doctrine, and beautiful), we have often forgotten his intimacy with the whole world. Worse, we forget that we have forgotten it. We feel uncomfortable sometimes in the presence of such thoughts—perhaps feeling guilty for looking for God as present in the wood and water and light around us as in our conceptions of heaven.

As in everything, balance is needed. Pantheism (the belief that "all is God") is counter to the Bible's vision of the Almighty. To a certain extent, bare panentheism ("God is in all") is contrary to the vision too, since the effect of such doctrine is to decentralize God's presence and minimize the truth that he is both transcendent, a being utterly beyond, and immanent, a being utterly here.

God is truly above and truly below. Utterly there and completely here and still outside of all such categories of space-time. In all places without diminishment or dilution yet in every age choosing to center his presence specially in particular places—a garden, a mountain, a tent, a temple, a man, a church aflame on Pentecost.

When we lose our sense of God's immanence, of his dwelling, even if invisibly, in sustaining power throughout all he has made, we forget this: that in every life we take of man or beast, in every natural place we mine or harvest, in every eye we gaze into or look away from, we encounter something utterly strange, utterly familiar, utterly sacred.

WE CHRISTIANS FORGET THE CLOSENESS THAT THE CREATOR OF ALL THINGS KEEPS WITH HIS CREATION.

Sacred I say, not only with its inherent worth as a thing once called "very good" by the voice of God but as a place where he lives and works at this very moment. We forget to approach all of creation with reverence for its Maker because we forget that he is truly closer than a brother, closer than our breath is to our throats, than our skin to our sinews.

Basil the Great, one of the most potent early theologians of the Spirit, said this of the everywhere-ness of the Spirit in creation. Basil wrote that God's Holy Spirit is

> boundless in power, unlimited in greatness, immea-
> surable by times or by aeons, bountiful in his

good gifts; unto whom all things turn when they
need holiness, whom all things long after that live
according to virtue.... Perfecting all others, himself
wanting in nothing, not living himself by removal
but the giver of life; not growing by accessions, but
at once complete, stablished in himself and existing
everywhere. The source of holiness; the intellectual light; giving to every rational power a certain
enlightenment from himself for the discovery of
truth. By nature unapproachable; comprehensible
by his own graciousness. Filling all things by his
power, yet communicable to the worthy alone. Not
communicated to all in the same measure, but dis-
tributing his energy according to the proportion of
faith. Uncompounded in his essence; various in his
powers. Wholly present to each, and wholly present
everywhere. Divided without passion; being shared,
yet remaining whole, like a ray of the sun, whose
favor to him who enjoys it is as if to him alone, but
which shines over land and sea, and is diffused into
the air. Even so the Holy Spirit, while he is wholly
present to every one capable of receiving him,
infuses into all a grace complete and sufficient, so
that partakers enjoy him according to the measure
of their ability, not of his power.[2]

Basil, in so brilliantly summing up the Bible's vision of the Spirit
as the all-present renewer of the earth, visualized a creation in which

every created thing is full to capacity with the creating and sustaining Spirit. Full, but only able to participate in the Spirit's life and reveal his power in keeping with the ability of their nature. In this way, all things reveal him, but only as far as they are able. Thus, a rock is full to capacity of God's Spirit who creates and sustains it, but can only enjoy and reveal the Spirit to the extent that a rock can enjoy and reveal anything. A deer or a tree is full to capacity of the sustaining sacred Spirit but is only able to show or know him as much as a deer or a tree can show or know anything. A child, a man, a redeemed man, an angel—all are able to know, to enjoy, to show, to reveal the Spirit who saturates them as the Spirit saturates all of creation, but are only able to do so in keeping with their nature, not in the Spirit's limitless power.

Meet the ever-present God, the renewing and sustaining Spirit.

What would it mean if this were true?

Would it mean that cutting the grass could be a sacred act? Might planting and harvesting transform from mundane toil into encounters of worship for the Creator's Spirit who sustains even the dormant grains in our fingers? Could the clandestine scattering of wildflower seeds in a ditch be a holy partnership with the one who makes even galaxies to bloom?

We would look at animals differently, would we not? Would we not view them as creatures limited in faculty but rich in value, worthy of holy kindness and respect? We would honor the Giver of all life, even with the arrow on our bowstring, even as we use their flesh and skin. We would, with Saint Francis, perhaps even find in the ravening wolves echoes of their Maker, that Spirit of love who sees fit to sustain predator and prey, bringing that dearest freshness deep down to even the fiercest of the creatures he has made.

We would begin to look on others of our own kind in the light of those "ah! bright wings." We might begin to cast off forever the broken ways that we exploit and judge and rate and devalue our brothers and sisters. For of all the mysteries of our physical world, all the life that the Holy Spirit has called up from carbon, all the family of breathing beings, humanity is the crown, the clearest unity of body and spirit, the form God himself chose to wear when the Creator himself became a thing that had been created.

WE WOULD LIVE WHOLEHEARTEDLY, SET
APART, MEMBERS OF A PRIESTLY KINGDOM,
IF WE LIVED AS IF THE SUSTAINER OF ALL
THINGS IS AS PRESENT IN OUR WORLD
AS OUR DOCTRINE TELLS US HE IS.

We would love differently, long differently, fight differently, make peace differently. We would grow differently, cultivate differently, prune differently, preen differently. We would make, unmake, remake, buy, and sell differently. Learn and teach, rest and work, look into every mirror differently.

Things that seem common now would be revealed as sacred— the pouring of a glass of pure water, the kindling of a fire in the woodstove, the entering of a newly built house for the first time. Blessedness would reveal itself—the full-breeding blessedness of a God ever present in glory, but who for his own reasons usually makes us uncover his face from the elements that veil his smile. A God who, even while building a house of worship in an eternal kingdom, can be found in a tree, on a mountain, in the loins of a light-footed deer panting for fresh water.

We would live wholeheartedly, set apart, members of a priestly kingdom, if we lived as if the sustainer of all things is as present in our world as our doctrine tells us he is.

So why don't we?

I hold up the fingers that type this page.

The nail of my right forefinger is creased with a white dash from an imprecise hammer strike last month. The back of one thumb has a smudge of ash from starting this morning's fire—soap and water didn't quite get rid of it before breakfast. There are scars—the gash from a folding knife when I was twelve or so, a moon-white jagged crescent in the meat of my left pointer from the faulty slide action of a little Beretta pistol, punched long ago when I was clearing a jammed cartridge while shooting soup cans in the woods. Light calluses from shovel and hatchet mar the base of my fingers, and more calluses, from playing guitar, harden the tips.

I turn them back and forth. Can it be that the Spirit is even now binding the cells and cartilage of these fingers, holding together all the parts that make them? If he ceased to speak a word or play a note, would they decay before my eyes? Are they merely a simple little melody in the great raucous chorus of creation that only exists for any span of anything because the Spirit who calls light out of darkness, everything out of nothing, world out of abyss, is still chanting the ancient tune?

My fingers look a bit like branches, and I remember that *etsem*, the Hebrew word for "bone," is a cousin to *ets*, the word for "tree."

Does the Spirit really murmur in them, these clever little twigs of bone? In knowing them, the scars of their bark, their markings of ash and oil, can I know him a little more? In knowing him, can I learn something of them?

But praising the Spirit of God as the sustainer, the renewer of earth, raises questions. It troubles those of us who recognize that nature is (as in Tennyson's famous verse in "In Memoriam"[3]) "red in tooth and claw." If all this creation is a note, a symphony, a thought even now actively sustained by the Spirit of creation, how do we account for the deaths, the red blood, the hanging trees? Yes, yes, the fall. It is the second-oldest story: the marring of God's "very good" creation by the sin of our race. "Through the Fall," wrote theologian Dumitru Stăniloae, "a motion toward divergence and decomposition entered creation. It is only through Christ, as God incarnate, that the parts of creation have begun to recompose themselves so as to make possible its future transfiguration, for from Christ the unifying and eternally living Spirit is poured out over creation."[4]

But can we dismiss the red so easily as that?

Annie Dillard, whose *Pilgrim at Tinker Creek* is one of the best books about God that I have ever read, wrote extensively of this. In one place, she observed:

> Sir James Jeans, British astronomer and physicist, suggested that the universe was beginning to look more like a great thought than a great machine. Humanists seized on the expression, but it was hardly news. We knew, looking around, that a thought branches and leafs, a tree comes to a conclusion. But the question of who is thinking the thought is more fruitful than the question of who made the machine, for a machinist can of course wipe his hands and leave, and his simple machine still hums; but if the thinker's attention strays for a minute, his simplest thought ceases altogether. And ... the place where we so incontrovertibly find ourselves, whether thought or machine, is at least not in any way simple.[5]

Not in any way simple, and the complexity, like Dillard's famous water bug, seems out to pierce the world with its proboscis, to suck the life and meaning from innocent frogs, from the universe.

On the one hand, we rejoice to hear words like those of the Puritan Walter Cradock, who said that "the Lord makes a Saint glad of a Primrose, of a little turning of the water"[6] because of his nearness to creation. But if this is true, can a saint also be glad of a nettle, a little burning of rattlesnake venom because of that same immanence, the same thought from the Divine Thinker?

If the Spirit is truly here, sustaining everything, close as breath and blood, then is he present in the lion's fangs as he tears flesh from the still-living gazelle? Is he present in the tracks of yellow bulldozers as they crush life from a rain forest for the profit of a few? Is he present in the thousand unnameable acts of cruelty, torture, murder, abuse, exploitation, and violence with which people, made in the image of their Maker, scar and sear and kill one another?

Is he in the hand of the wicked?

Does God's Spirit sustain even them?

As we stretch ourselves to span the apparent gaps between the Spirit's perfection and holiness and his intimate presence in a brutal world, we must either grow through faith or snap, like the backbones of rabbits, from a lack of it.

We are under deep waters.

Could it be that the Holy Spirit's continued presence, continued grace to sustain, even as the creation he holds up yelps and whimpers and ravens and groans for new birth, could it be that this is the grace of God? Could his sustaining work highlight his utter kindness, his patience, his willingness to be wronged and grieved by the things he has made?

In *O Death, Where Is Thy Sting?*, Alexander Schmemann wrote:

> Indeed, people continue dying as they did before,
> and the world continues to be filled with separa-
> tions, with sadness and suffering. But within that

world there has been ignited and continues to burn the light of faith. It is not simply a belief that somewhere, at some point beyond the confines of this life, our existence will continue … [b]ut in the fact that the world itself and life itself have once more received purpose and meaning.[7]

Purpose and meaning! The world of the immanent Spirit never lost it, but it takes on fresh meaning for a fallen humanity being redeemed, re-created, renewed. For in that immanent Spirit, Schmemann continued, "There is no more loneliness, there is no more fear and darkness. I am with you, says Christ, I am with you now and always, with complete love, with all knowledge, with all power."[8]

We try to swing here, to span the gaps. But God is also reaching, bridging, drawing the poles together.

I have questions. I do not have answers.

Perhaps the best that I can do is to cite the end of Tennyson's bloody stanza:

> *O for thy voice to soothe and bless!*
> *What hope of answer, or redress?*
> *Behind the veil, behind the veil.*[9]

We must have faith that the soothing, the blessing, is closer than the harm and will outlast it. The truth, hard to wait for, and a perilous trail to walk, is this: there is hope of answer, and redress.

Behind the veil? Perhaps. But the veil is thinner than our skin.

To twist Tennyson a bit more:

> *Peace; come away: we do him wrong*
> *To sing so wildly: let us go.*[10]

Perhaps this struggle is what puts the real strength into the doctrine of God's everywhere-ness through the Spirit. If he were not present in every pain and loss, near to us in every crime and suffering, then how, at the end of all things, could he judge righteously? C. S. Lewis noted the madness of Christ, who (I paraphrase) seemed to be convinced that all wrongs were wrongs committed against himself. Megalomania, or omnipresence through the Spirit of Jesus?

There may never be a quieting, on this side of the veil at least, of these questions. For some of the most difficult mysteries, we can only seek to find stasis, perhaps the deep peace that surpasses understanding in their presence, being wholly unable to make them go away.

Of God's omnipresence, A. W. Tozer wrote:

> This great central truth gives meaning to all other truths and imparts supreme value to all [man's] little life. God is present, near him, next to him, and this God sees him and knows him through and through.
>
> At this point faith begins.[11]

God the Holy Spirit is present. Near. Here. Next to. Seeing, knowing, known according to ability and revelation. In all things sustaining, still calling for the very good even in the presence of the very bad. About us, amid us, among us, and all the following prepositions.

The Present One is patient.

Faith begins.

Saint Basil said of the Spirit:

> He it is who holds the earth, grasping it with His hands. He has arranged all things in order; He set the mountains in their places and measured the waters. He assigns to each thing in the universe its proper rank.... The cause of being comes from Him to all things that exist, according to the will of God the Father. Through Him structure and preservation are given to all things, for He created everything, and dispenses well-being to all things, according to the need of each. Therefore all things are turned toward Him, looking with irresistible longing and unspeakable love to the creator and sustainer of life.[12]

Are we turned toward him? Have we felt the love and the longing for the source of all life, that strange polar magnetism that pulls our hearts toward the burning Someone who rests and flutters in every root and branch and bloom of the world? Do we live in turning toward him, turning our work and every relationship with the whole of the created and sustained world into worship of the one from whom all comes and to whom all returns? Or have we dared to forget the very one who at this moment wills us to be and to become? Have we dared to forget the one whose eternal yes to the world is all that holds any of us above the face of the deep?

HE HATES NOTHING THAT HE HAS MADE, NO MATTER HOW THE DARKNESS HOWLS. BUT HE IS NOT CONTENT TO LET BROKENNESS REMAIN FOREVER.

We turn to him, return to him with what we learn from him—the strange unspoken love, the welcome, the joy of the dear freshness at the deep center of things. Though the cedars may break, and all this marred and cutting world bare its claws at you, here is truth: the wind that rends the limbs of the ancient trees is a wind of love, fierce and beyond full knowing, but knowable still, warm with God's radiant affection for all things. Warm with affection for us.

In God's sustaining, as in his creation, the old words can be heard, echoing forever across the rippling water: *It's good that you are; how wonderful that you exist!* The Creator and Sustainer made everything in love and he keeps everything in love.

He hates nothing that he has made, no matter how the darkness howls.

But he is not content to let brokenness remain forever.

"Grant it, I beseech thee," runs an old Armenian liturgical prayer to the Holy Spirit, "that thy divinity may be everywhere revealed in all things, and glorified with the Father and the Son with equal honor."[13] Amen and amen.

Puritan preacher Walter Cradock, whom I quoted earlier, wrote beautifully of the sentiment that he wished his church members could express in relation to the Holy Spirit's revelation of himself. He wished they could say,

> God hath appeared two hundred times, two thousand times to my soule. I have seene him one while in the Sacrament, I have seen him among the Saints, I have seene him in such a country, in such a condition, in such a place, in such a medow, in such a wood, when I read his word, and called upon his name.[14]

And so, I will say it, here in my home at the edge of the burned forest, where on the flowering of a lush spring day I look through my window at the trees breaking, as if for the first time, into a new year's growth.

God hath appeared two hundred times to my soule.

I have seen the Spirit in the bread and wine of Christ's table.

I have seen him in the waters of baptism.

I have seen him in the church, in the holy oil placed on the heads of the faithful, in the clay eyes of the homeless.

I have seen him in a child's hair, in the water of the creek by my kitchen.

I have seen him in the discarded syringes that littered my old neighborhood in east Portland.

I saw him in the closed eyes of my baby brother as he died, and in the opening eyes of my daughter and sons as they were born.

I have seen him in yellowed paper, in tanned leather, in carved wood, in cast iron.

I have seen him in tulip and crocus blooms.

I have seen him in lamb's wool and lamb's-quarters.

I have seen him in the canals of Venice, in the stones of Jerusalem, in Banksy's holy graffiti on the military walls of Palestine.

I have seen him as children burned piled tires in a Roma village in Croatia.

I have seen him buried in a stone graveyard in Providence.

I saw him in the lights of New York as I passed on the expressway, in the fireflies of the Blue Ridge Mountains, in the prairie grass west of Chicago.

I have seen him in the sacred Black Hills and in the birdlike oil rigs bobbing near Casper, Wyoming.

I have seen him in Da Vinci's *Vitruvian Man*, in the impasto of Van Gogh's olive trees, in the blue whores of Toulouse-Lautrec.

I saw him flutter at twilight once, outside the mouth of Ape Cave, and rise at dawn (disguised as a raven) from the white oak by the train tracks.

I saw him in the mist rising in the forest near Eagle Creek (but you knew that already), and in the blown-glass Christmas ornaments that hung on my grandmother's tree.

I saw him once in a cracked tile at the bottom of a green swimming pool, once in the steam that rose from fresh peppermint tea.

I have seen him tinkering away in the particle accelerators of Fermilab, flashing in the motion of monorails, refracting in the headlights of taxicabs.

ALL OF EVERYTHING IS A SYMPHONY, AND NO CREATED THING HAS EVER HEARD THE FULLNESS OF IT.

I have seen him on the stone stairs to nowhere in the ghost town where I live.

I have seen him in the bodies of my beloved dead as we laid them in the earth with roses, and in the warm hands of my beloved living as we laughed and embraced at a hundred birthdays.

I have seen him in April lilacs, in a handful of dust, in the fire, in the rose, in the apple tree, in the hidden waterfall.

I have seen him in you.

Notes all, we ring, sustained, vibrating forever. Listen! All of everything is a symphony, and no created thing has ever heard the fullness of it. All of it, all of us, somehow, he renews, now and for eternity. The cedars break at his voice, but he replants them, every one.

Do you hear music?

POURED ON ALL FLESH

Rejoicing in the Spirit of New Things

Waiting.
Pacing back and forth.
Expecting.
Charting the heavens.
Waiting for a sign.
Perhaps a star.

—Martin Bell, *The Way of the Wolf*

I will pour out my spirit on all flesh;
your sons and your daughters shall prophesy,
your old men shall dream dreams,
and your young men shall see visions.
Even on the male and female slaves,
in those days, I will pour out my spirit.
I will show portents in the heavens and on the earth.

—Joel 2:28–30

When I was a boy, the farm we lived on had a few acres of billowing grass in a pasture on the north end of our sheet-metal machine shed. The land was bordered and bisected by several generations of dilapidated fences—the posts and tangled wires looking like some halfhearted defense misplaced from the World War I trenches.

One booted foot through a rusty loop, my other up over the barricade, and over I'd go, like a soldier, thigh-deep into the grass and Queen Anne's lace. In summer, field mice burrowed through dry tunnels of stems that arched over the dirt, their trails overlooked by grasshoppers that chewed the green stalks above, and by the praying mantises that chewed the green grasshoppers. Among them, killdeers nested, feinting battle wounds for the boy who came too close, dragging a falsely broken wing to distract from a nest of mottled eggs disguised like pebbles in the dirt.

Many are the long days that I would look at the grasses of the fields, thinking that there should be a dozen words for them, to reflect their different widths and lengths of blade, their varying propensities to slice fingers that grip them, the myriad shades of green and bowed brown, their reedy voices under a stiff breeze. How simple a thing a meadow is, only earth and grasses and the inhabitants of earth and grasses, and yet in it, invisible to all but children and farmers, plays the sustained drama of life.

As a child I loved the Bible, reading it for hours in our red farmhouse that looked out on this field. I would think of the verses that compare human life to the life of grasses, transient and fleeting, green one day and a husk the next. *As below, so above*, I thought, and wondered if the earth itself might have the same manner of life span, grassy, here and gone again, in spite of its ancientness by our reckoning.

Perhaps, I speculated, our whole solar system was only a field, a meadow of ancient void, appearing as dust and cold when viewed by short-lived eyes like mine, but in reality teeming with life on a different scale, where a heartbeat lasted a millennia. Perhaps the asteroid fields and nebulae were the bisecting fences of the dancing green, the comets so many burrowing rodents under the lawn, the planets dancers on the grass, moons and rings akimbo, in a folk dance whose steps can only be perceived as astronomical equations. Virginia reels danced on the Milky Way.

It was in this place beyond the fences, occupied with thoughts like this, that I first understood what it meant that "the heavens opened."

I was lying in the grasses of that north pasture on a summer day. All was warm and dry. The air was alive with sound, the pulse of insects and bird calls. Above me the clouds navigated in cotton fleets, like symmetrical battleships. The haze of the Oregon summer light textured the whole world. This day the movement of the clouds seemed to function as a bellows for some unseen fire behind things. "Glory be to God for dappled things,"[1] Hopkins wrote, and glory all the more to God for moments like this one— the whole world seemed to rise up, dappled and brindled, flecked like pyrite.

The sunlight flared, took on the quality of old photographs. I got up and stood there, an awkward kid in green rubber boots and high-water pants, watching the world emerge like a butterfly from its cocoon. Then the magic of the one light gave way to yet another. Clouds of a second layer that I did not even know had been there dissolved. The brightness became something more than natural.

I looked up.

In that field I saw—not learned, *saw*—for the first time that our sun is a great star. It looked so glorying in the sky above our planet like a bridegroom with his beloved. It had turned the color of true fire, the inestimable fire of space, able to blind and burn my kind from a distance of nearly ninety-three million miles. It warmed me and comforted me and made me afraid. It was as if day turned to glorious night, a night of stars in a blue sky.

For a moment I thought this was the true dawn, the end, the beginning, the second coming of Christ. The re-creation. I really did—for a moment I thought it was the end of the world. I raised my hands. My heart leaped in the field like a small soldier or a little shaking lamb. I was happy and afraid.

We each make an assumption about the world that defines how we look at it. This assumption is our view of history—it influences choices, joy, and despair, our conceptions of worth, of humanity, of God.

We can think about time in two ways. One way is to think of it as a circle or a spiraling series of circles, drawing the story of humanity and the cosmos through the same essential motions, actions, and reactions. To those who think this way, the universe is part of an eternal cycle of birth, death, and rebirth. Undoubtedly this way of thinking has beauty but also horror—in most of the old pagan stories, even the gods cannot stop their own cycles of birth and death, and the world is fated, her dance written unchangeably, spinning her like a child's top over a grooved course she's traced countless times before. Direction? Nothing has any real direction. No call to the cosmic dancers could change a single step or misstep, for all that is has been, and will fall and will be again, only to fall again. In such a philosophy, any of us is at best a happy human-colored blur as the globe whirls beneath us.

WE WANT TO LIVE IN A WORLD
WHERE *NEW* MEANS SOMETHING.

The other way is to conceive of history as some sort of line—a road, a path. This, of course, allows for movement, for forwardness, for the possibilities of growth, evolution, revolution, and progress. For the possibility of leaving a chapter of history behind, never to open it again. For the possibility to open a chapter that will never close. Patterns may repeat, but never history itself, and the terms *old* and *new* carry real meaning, for the fabric of reality allows them to.

The Christian conception, the only conception with hope, is the second way of thinking about time.

We want to live in a world where *new* means something.

To expect the end of the world is human. All thinkers and faiths do it in their own way, whether as a section of the circle or a point on the line.

From the best guesses of scientists paid to study such things, the earth will end (in roughly 7.5 billion years) in a fiery absorption into the sun, gobbled up by jolly Papa Sol long after our planet has been dead and barren for eons. Think of it! The star of life will become the star of death. It will look, from the bare bedrock of the place that was once a field that I stood in, as if the sun is truly descending. Light will change to light, heat to heat, and the elements will consume themselves.

Other scientists posit that not merely our planet, but the universe itself has a life span—having blown outward over the ages of ages, it will at some point hang for a breathy, motionless millisecond, then contract back on itself like the wave of all things rushing to shore, back to the original moment of creation.

Rather apocalyptic.

Christianity, of course, is an apocalyptic faith at its core. We expect God, at a time unknowable by humans or by angels, to break into our current reality with unprecedented clarity, like the sun dissipating every cloud to recolor the whole world.

Christianity's deepest vision of apocalypse is unique, a new beginning through the Spirit. Not merely an end, not merely a restoration, even. A true *beginning*. Our Bible has an entire genre of literature, aptly termed *apocalyptic*, that uses wild symbolism, numerology, and visions of past and future to communicate the meaning behind God's plan for the world today and tomorrow. These visions of prophets and apostles whirl with color and impossible creatures. Beasts who are kingdoms arise from the sea. Dragons sweep the stars from heaven with their tails. The dead plead before the throne of the Almighty. The Lamb who was dead yet lives rules the universe as a king.

OURS, YOU SEE, IS A FAITH OF NEW THINGS. OURS IS A FAITH OF NEW CREATION, NEW BEGINNING.

Apocalypse, from the Greek word ἀποκάλυψις (*apokalupsis*), simply means "revelation," literally, an "uncovering." The veil (all veils perhaps) between our reality and whatever is above and behind and after it is lifted. For all the wild brutality, all the monstrosity of image and story in the biblical writings that we call "apocalyptic," thinking of them as truly the end of the world is not only inaccurate but is counter-Christian.

The world is not ended in Christian theology. Ever. Instead, it is revealed in its truest, restored, and "very good" form. *Apocalypse.* The Christian view of the end, for all the destruction of its symbolism, is remarkable, gently reframing what it would mean for our world to end. Apocalyps-ized. Uncovered. A veil is torn, top to bottom, from heaven to earth, uncovering the holy place that was always behind it.

Ours, you see, is a faith of new things. Ours is a faith of new creation, new beginning. Revelations. Apocalypse.

The end of the world. The work of the Spirit.

The writer of Isaiah 43 said:

> Thus says the LORD,
>> who makes a way in the sea,
>> a path in the mighty waters ...
> Do not remember the former things,
>> or consider the things of old.
> I am about to do a new thing;
>> now it springs forth, do you not perceive it?
> I will make a way in the wilderness. (vv. 16,
>> 18–19)

The God who has always called us out—from the ancient waters, from bondage, from oppression and fear and violence—this God promises to make a path, leading us to the water of life in the wilderness. He promises to pour out drink for his people in the desert.

God is the great doer of new things, leading us ever to what is good for us, even if the trail there has not yet been blazed. It is this newness that echoes out from the words spoken by the Spirit of creation above the face of the deep; the newness that shines in the work of the hand, in the word of the mouth, in the surprise of a God who can work in speech and in silence, in the shocking fresh green of a sprouting stump, in the dear freshness the Renewer of Earth brings to all things.

In that, we come to Joel.

While all Christians have awaited the second coming of Jesus (the true and ultimate apocalypse), it is in Joel's prophecy that God's love of new things bears the richest promise.

> I will pour out my spirit on all flesh;
> your sons and your daughters shall prophesy,
> your old men shall dream dreams,
> and your young men shall see visions.
> Even on the male and female slaves,
> in those days, I will pour out my spirit.
> I will show portents in the heavens and on the
> earth. (Joel 2:28–30)

There is this thing about God. He is a God, someone once said, "who makes promises and keeps them," and while this is true (he is the ultimate promise maker, the ultimate truth teller), in his love and wisdom he rarely fulfills his promise in the way we expect. It is always stranger, out of step with the world's dance, in resounding echo only to his own internal, perfect rhythm. He steps among us on the dancing green, clapping, syncopated, calling his steps a few moves before his feet fall, but in spite of the warning, the movements are always a surprise, stranger and more beautiful than we expected.

Jesus was the grand flourish of his dance, a sweeping footwork in tune with no known melody, but reminding us of every beautiful thing the Spirit has ever done. Strange and good.

The Jews of Christ's time wanted a militant messiah—a zealot warrior come with a sword for Roman necks in one hand and bread for Jewish bellies in the other. They got exactly that, but because God was doing a new thing, the sword was not the sword they longed for, and neither was the bread.

The steps of every dancer were being upset by God's Spirit, transformed in the light of the descending sun.

It was a new thing.

Joel is a book of apocalypse. It begins with a plague of green grasshoppers that strip the Promised Land bare of every growing thing. They bring famine, fear, destruction. Joel is a book of invasion, of alarm trumpets, of clouds and gloom and thick darkness. It is a book of portents, the very sun turning to darkness in the sky.

But the horrors all highlight God's promises through the prophet. He promises unprecedented justice, redemption, deliverance. And the centerpiece of the little prophetic leaflet is the pouring out of the Spirit.

✴ ✴ ✴ ✴ ✴ ✴ ✴

GOD IS THE GREAT DOER OF NEW
THINGS, LEADING US EVER TO WHAT
IS GOOD FOR US, EVEN IF THE TRAIL
THERE HAS NOT YET BEEN BLAZED.

"I will pour out my Spirit on all flesh," God said. He was addressing a culture that understood the work of God among humanity as mediated work—to the people through a prophet, a priest, a king. Poured out on *all?* This was a new thing.

"All flesh," God said—then Joel's expansive elaboration, leaving no one out: "your sons … your daughters … your old men … your young men … even your male and female slaves." Every type of person is represented in Joel's vision—male and female, old and young, all the way to what the Hebrews considered the lowest of society, the slaves, who by law were mostly foreign born. Beyond divisions of ethnicity, age, gender, wealth. On them, on all, the Spirit was to be poured out. God's promise was for apocalypse, for the world turned upside down. Through the Spirit, he was talking about the end of the world as we know it.

A new thing.

In Acts 2, on the day of Pentecost when the Holy Spirit descended in wind and fire on the followers of Jesus in Jerusalem, Peter said that the prophecy of Joel was being fulfilled. Full of the Spirit, Christ's brash disciple

> raised his voice and addressed them, "Men of Judea
> and all who live in Jerusalem, let this be known to
> you, and listen to what I say …. This is what was
> spoken through the prophet Joel:
> 'In the last days it will be, God declares,
> that I will pour out my Spirit upon all flesh,
>   and your sons and your daughters shall
>   prophesy,

and your young men shall see visions,

and your old men shall dream dreams.

Even upon my slaves, both men and women,

in those days I will pour out my Spirit;

and they shall prophesy.

And I will show portents in the heaven above

and signs on the earth below,

blood, and fire, and smoky mist.

The sun shall be turned to darkness

and the moon to blood,

before the coming of the Lord's great and

glorious day.

Then everyone who calls on the name of the Lord

shall be saved.'" (vv. 14, 16–21)

Peter said that when the Spirit was poured out, the world was seeing its last days. Confusing, perhaps, because history has obviously continued, but *true*—all things were beginning to end. It was the apocalypse. The end of the world had truly come. *Has* truly come, by the Spirit, who at once was a descending fire of judgment (but not the judgment we expected) and the poured-out promise beginning to flow over all flesh. This was the vision that Joel saw.

What do Peter's words mean? That the last days are *these* days, *our* days. The day of the boy in the field. The day of the dancers. We have lived in the last days ever since the Spirit fell to indwell the church with power. Ever since Pentecost we have lived at the end of the world. But it has not been the end that we expected. Because

God is doing a new thing, the fire of the apocalypse that fell from heaven to end the world was not the fire of destruction. It was the fire of the Holy Spirit. God began to end the world on Pentecost, began a new chapter of making all things new.

EVER SINCE PENTECOST WE HAVE LIVED AT THE END OF THE WORLD. BUT IT HAS NOT BEEN THE END THAT WE EXPECTED.

Who knows what the true dawn will bring? We still await Christ's coming in glory, the rise and descent of the Sun of Righteousness, empowered by the Spirit to transform and burn alive and purify. But according to Joel and Peter, that burning and transforming have already started.

Who could have said they expected God's fiery dance to look like this?

The gift of God to every generation of Christians is that they should be the last to live on the earth. There will come, I believe, a moment of utter end, though the details of that day are mysterious, but that does not lessen the power of this fact: none of us know the day or hour, and we all are allowed full expectation. The end could come today. It could have come every one of two thousand years of yesterdays. It might come after two thousand years of tomorrows.

It is, I say, a gift of God to be able to look at the sky every day and wonder, *Maybe today*. This is the gift of the Spirit who does new things, who is able to do new things, who has done new things, who is even now *doing* new things. Every contemplation of the end is a contemplation of a beginning. He makes it so. He has already been poured out on all flesh, already ended the world as it was, and though he often is hidden, he washes over the world like a wave of new lamp oil waiting to be set alight.

No one knows the hour that the sky will truly open, the veil torn in a way that the eye can see. Every Christian, from baptism until death, has watched the skies in accordance with our teaching, looking for the fulfillment of Scripture and the creeds. Truly, we await his coming in glory.

EVERY CONTEMPLATION OF THE END IS A CONTEMPLATION OF A BEGINNING.

But the glory is that, in one sense, we await the one who is already here. The Spirit has been poured out on us as representatives of and ambassadors to all flesh. Our glory and gift is to be the last, the very last, to see around us, as the Spirit is poured out on us, even the most unexpected of us, the signs and the portents.

We are the last. So were Paul and Peter, Polycarp and Perpetua, John the Golden Mouth, Saint Patrick, Julian of Norwich, Susanna Wesley and her sons, D. L. Moody, Elizabeth of the Trinity, Watchman

Nee, Martin Luther King Jr. Old men, young women. Rich, poor. Of every background.

Here, at the ever-present end of the world, the light of the Spirit grows and glows, and is glorious. My heart leaps in the field like a small soldier or a little shaking lamb. The stars spin.

The Spirit is here. He pours himself out. I have seen visions.

I am happy and afraid.

Part 2
SEVEN LAMPSTANDS

THE DOVE OF THE BELOVED

Believing the Spirit of Unconditional Love

Dove: Immanuel, God with us in our flesh.
Eagle: What is that? Is he in our flesh?
Dove: He is, if we are in his Spirit.

—Morgan Llwyd, *Llyfr y tri Aderyn*

Just as [Jesus] was coming up out of the water, he saw
the heavens torn apart and the Spirit descending like a
dove on him. And a voice came from heaven, "You are
my Son, the Beloved; with you I am well pleased."

—Mark 1:10–11

I kept running around it in large or small circles, always looking
for someone or something able to convince me of my Belovedness.

—Henri Nouwen, *Life of the Beloved*

Do you remember being a child?

The natural state of children is one of nearly total imagination. As little ones grow out of toddlerhood, they enter a world that looks identical on the surface to that which adults live in, but which in reality is a place of wonder, terror, magic, and grand adventure.

143

Adults never quite recapture the innocent ease, the way that children effortlessly paint their world in imagination. Which of your grown-up friends could you picture standing knee-deep in the creek outside the kitchen door, swirling dirt and water in a blue camping mug, and offering you "hot chocolate"? Which of them have you caught trying to undress in a tree on a frigid day because they had inadvertently become a monkey? Or which have taken a running leap into you, shocked that they didn't simply fly up, up, and away over you?

For children, anything can become anything, and it frequently does. If adults live like this, we call them mad or artists or prophets, and seek them treatment, give them colored pills. If children do it, we call them clever or cute or brilliant, and seek them new playthings, give them colored paintbrushes.

While kids are still being daily lifted and fed, their clothes put on them and taken off of them, while they are still helpless in so many basic ways, it is then that their imagination is most vibrantly alive. They may not be able to run without tripping, but they can fly faster than airplanes. They may not be able to put on lipstick like mama, but they can become royalty who dress in silk, dripping with diamonds, attended by fairies. They may not be able to carry the steak knives to set the table, but they can wield jagged swords and cutlasses, giving no quarter to their enemies. The small and powerless grow in a moment to fill the universe.

This life of the imagination is nearly omnipotent, and so I wonder if the life of children brushes closer to the Spirit's experience of reality than anything that adults can easily remember. God, for whom to think, to speak a word is to cause to become, seems to me deliciously childlike. We call him the Ancient of Days, and so he is, but if he is infinitely ancient (that is, eternal), then he is no less infinitely young (also eternal).

In the end, could it be that the "faith of a little child" is just a phrase for imagination pointed in the most Godward direction? To butcher Longfellow, perhaps God's "will is the wind's will, and the thoughts of youth are long, long thoughts."[1] But, adults might say, then we have to grow up, to put away childish things, to mature.

We forget, though, that the Spirit's definition of maturity may not be our own.

If you were a being limitless in power, bound by nothing but your own being, infinite in joy and imagination, and intent on concentrating yourself for a flickering moment at a particular point of space and time, what form would you take?

Think of it! You could become a multitude, a revelation, an anything woven from sheer glory and unopposable will. No product of your limitless imagination would be beyond your grasp.

And … you choose a dove, symbol of simplicity, peace, deliverance, meekness. You center yourself to become small, to flutter. You move over your own creation as a little fragile bit of your own great call into being.

What does that say about you, Holy Spirit, you great thing feathered with wonder?

In that moment, as you looked from above, down into your own eyes in the brown face of a carpenter from Nazareth, standing in the brown Jordan River below, as you heard your own voice, the Father's voice speaking from you, from outside you, from far above you, what would you feel for the you that was also the them, your Beloved?

And do you feel that today, for all those being made in Jesus after your kind?

How many different loves there are in the world! It is foolish that we who speak English use the same word for them all.

The love of a father and a mother for a child.

A love for tamed animals, still another for wild ones, a love that seems specific toward birds and all things that fly.

A kind of love for new places, and a different kind for *our* places; a love for the homes that we have known, and a yearning, sharp variety (the Welsh call it *hiraeth*) for the love of a home we have never yet known.

A love of ice and snowpack, a different love of fire and ember. Different loves still of the earth and of the air, of the inner spirit.

A love that rises between kindred spirits, and a complementary love shared by people of profound difference.

A love of ironwork and stonemasonry and all difficult, cold, and unforgiving crafts; and a love of the garden, of leatherwork, wood, and pottery, and of all warm, welcoming crafts.

A love that is faithful in spite of everything, and a love that is innocent and free, having never yet been tested.

A love felt for an enemy.

A love of long limbs and nakedness, indescribable, between one and a lover.

The love of the worshipper, the love of the worshipped, the love of the intercessor, and the love of the one being pled for.

The love of the Father, the love of the Son, the love of the Holy Spirit, the Dove of heaven.

The love of the Beloved.

I must stop, or I will write the entire world.

Other languages than mine carry a bit more nuance—C. S. Lewis popularized the "four loves"[2] of the Greeks, whose categories (*affection, friendship, eros,* and *charity*) help show the gradients of meaning that arise when we speak of this mystery.

The Bible's categories of love largely overlap with Lewis's. The *agape* love, so often cited by pastors, and the centerpiece of Paul's famous "love chapter," 1 Corinthians 13, is certainly the "unconditional" love of God but is also a love that is possible for us to understand, indeed, by God's power, to *replicate* in imitation of him. Though it is the closest that language can come to capturing God's love, and thus, God's nature, it is the audacious belief of Christians that such divine love is accessible to humanity. We can receive it. We can know when we have received it. Being made into the image of our Maker by the Spirit, we can begin to give it in turn.

You can love and be loved forever with the very love of God.

It is that unconditional but knowable *agape* love that the "Beloved" Jesus felt during his baptism in the Jordan. The Greek term is α'γαπητο'ς, (*agapétos*), "beloved." Whatever the Father experienced in looking upon his only begotten Son in that moment, it included full acceptance, deep pleasure, the love that gives and gives and gives of itself. It was the unreserved "very good" of God, spoken to the uncreated Son who was sharing his nature with created humanity, the "very good" of a beginning re-creation.

At that moment, above the waters of Jesus's baptism, the Trinity was present—the Father, speaking his joy from above, the eternal Son made flesh bathing in the slow Jordan, and the Holy Spirit, seen by Jesus coming down from heaven in the form of a dove. Here, at the moment he was to begin his public ministry, Jesus of Nazareth knew his full acceptance, the full delight of the everlasting community of the Trinity. He knew, beyond doubt, through the evidence of sense and nature, that he was the Father's Beloved.

YOU CAN LOVE AND BE LOVED FOREVER WITH THE VERY LOVE OF GOD.

The Spirit fluttered down. The holy wings that had whipped up the first black waters of the world and called them into light rustled over the carpenter from Nazareth. And like the dove that Noah sent out at the first watery death of the earth, the dove that first found no place suitable to perch, but later found a tree rising from the water, the Dove of heaven found the Tree of Jesse rising from the second waters, the old Creator made a new creation, dripping with life, beginning to remake the world, carrying in himself the seeds of perfect second life.

The Beloved life.

Your life, if you will have it, and mine.

In that moment, the Spirit can be most clearly seen as what he truly is—a blessing for the Beloved, a sign and seal and means of belovedness. The imagination of the Spirit was bent in the ancient direction—utter love—intersecting time and space to meet Jesus in the Jordan.

What did it mean for Jesus to be God's Beloved? When the Father spoke this in concert with the descending Spirit, it meant far more than "the son whom I really like." For Jesus to be God's beloved meant that in that moment, all the speakings of God to his people Israel as the beloved—the poetry of God, the longing of God for a righteous and holy family, all the promises and covenants and graces and blessings—rested on one representative of his people, indeed, of all of humanity. In Jesus rested the distilled belovedness of all of history. For the first time in history, humanity (under God's Spirit) had sent up a shoot, a sprout suitable for God, the Dove of heaven himself, to rest on without hesitation. For Jesus to be the Beloved meant that the Spirit was witnessing and sealing the ultimate definition of humanity, redefining maturity and imagination, and all that we think makes us. He simply accepted, simply came down in love on the beloved Son.

For Jesus to be the Beloved included his worthiness but was predicated on a choice beyond worthiness, in the same manner that any sane father is unable to keep back his love from his begotten. For Jesus to be the Beloved meant that all the longings of God for humanity and all the longings of humanity for God were concentrating themselves at a single point in the entire fabric of space-time, a point occupied by Christ, the God-man, the partaker of two natures, the bridge, the overlap, the extension and coextension. The union. The blessed and anointed head of the body that was to come.

THIS IS THE SPIRIT, GIVEN AND GIVING, UNION OF LOVER AND BELOVED. THIS IS THE LIFE GOD WANTS TO SHARE WITH YOU AT THIS MOMENT, AND FOR ALL ETERNITY.

For Jesus to be the Beloved meant that because he was a perfect representative, completely God and completely man, there was nothing keeping the love of the one from the love of the other. The Spirit could descend, a blessing, a resounding "yes!," the rejoicing of God who had longed from time immemorial to give himself without reservation to those who carried his image.

This is the Spirit, given and giving, union of Lover and beloved.

This is the life God wants to share with you at this moment, and for all eternity.

Pablo Picasso said:

> Each second we live is a new and unique moment
> of the universe, a moment that will never be again.
> And what do we teach our children? We teach them
> that two and two make four, and that Paris is the
> capital of France. When will we also teach them
> what they are? We should say to each of them: Do
> you know what you are? You are a marvel. You are
> unique. In all the years that have passed, there has
> never been another child like you.[3]

He nearly captures the wonder of being, of complete and unique existence. He nearly captures the blessing of belovedness. "It's good that you are; how wonderful that you exist!"

We should teach children, those imaginers of glories; we should teach and train them at every meal and during every game on the floor or in the grass that they are the beloved of God. They, we, *all* of us, through some mystery of divine action, can be seen by God as standing with Jesus in the river, receiving the affirmation and joy of the Trinity, intersecting the life of ultimate and terminal love.

Yes, we are a marvel, but for much more than merely our own uniqueness. We are a marvel because Christ is a marvel, and we can be just like our Older Brother if we long to be.

We can be the place where the Dove is pleased to perch.

Every second and moment that passes can be a place for the Dove of heaven to roost on *me*, if I am willing to see those places, to *be* those places. Will I let the Dove find a place to rest his foot? Will I learn to see the world and myself as the Great Seer does?

How many times I have shrugged off the foot of God! Through sin, through insecurity, through ignorance, through foolishness, how many times I have failed to know that I am, simply and without condition, God's beloved in Jesus through the Holy Spirit.

BELIEVING THAT WE ARE THE BELOVED OF GOD IS ONE OF THE MOST DIFFICULT THINGS WE COULD EVER DO.

This truth changes everything, transforms life from mere existence into the very presence of God, which, in spite of all appearances, makes earth, here and now, *heaven*. If we do not realize this, our values will be skewed, we will be blinded by the way things look rather than the way they are. We will not receive the deepest truth about ourselves, and therefore we cannot live it.

We smile to hear such words, smile and nod. But today we will all go on to remind each other, and each other's children, that two and two make four and that Paris is the capital of France. We will forget that belovedness is spoken over us. It is not conditional. It is *agape*, and we with Christ are *agapétos*. Beloved.

Because of our inner brokenness, believing that we are the beloved of God is one of the most difficult things we could ever do. Not becoming the beloved, mind you (this is the lie that nearly all of us believe), but *believing* it. Beyond any work of holiness or sacrifice, beyond any endeavor of faith, any struggle of doubt, the fight to simply accept this truth can be overwhelming. If, somehow, the Spirit does begin to intrude on our typical routine of striving and earning, the door he opens to enter seems to let in a dozen scurrying insecurities.

Am I the beloved—the liar, the vain, the lustful? Me, the impatient, the haughty, the angry, the lazy, the fool? I am willing to go under the Jordan, sure—returning to the waters that I came from makes sense—but am I willing to truly be raised into new life, to believe that the living water and the heavens have parted, and that God looks on me in kindness and in pleasure, choosing to see his own eyes, the eyes of Jesus the God-man, looking back at him from my face?

God may love me. He has to, right? But does he *like* me? Does he *delight* in me? Am I truly the beloved? Am I accepted by the Father, blessed under the wings of the Dove of heaven?

When God sees me, does he see something to love beyond condition, beyond earning?

Did he truly love us, as Paul wrote, before we loved him? We smile and nod but hardly ever believe it.

We lack the childlike, godlike imagination to believe it.

After all, in the "real world," two and two make four, and Paris is the capital of France.

This all reminds me of a section from one of Thomas Merton's letters. The passage is written to a "man of the world," who was corresponding by mail with the monk, a man who was deeply struggling with his unworthiness before God. Merton wrote to him:

> God is … the Seer and the Seeing and the Seen. God seeks Himself in us, and the aridity and sorrow of our heart is the sorrow of God who is not known in us, who cannot yet find Himself in us because we do not dare to believe or to trust the incredible truth that He could live in us, and live there out of choice, out of preference…. We exist solely for this, to be the place He has chosen for His presence, His manifestation in the world, His epiphany. But we make all this dark and inglorious because we fail to believe it, we refuse to believe it.[4]

Jesus, the Beloved, was seen by the Father, by the Spirit. For all the weakness of form that the Word made flesh took on, he was loved in wholeness, in totality, in truth. He, the Cornerstone, was laid there in the river. We all are being built into a temple around him, a place for joyous glory, for his Spirit like a dove to descend on and to reside within. A place for God to rest. That is very good.

Through the righteousness of Jesus the Beloved, we are "very good." In some mystery of paradoxical grace, God chooses to find himself in us.

Scripture, particularly Paul's theology, is clear that all of us "in Christ" are … *in Christ*. When God looks at his people and at all the individual members of his people, he chooses to see the face of his Beloved. No manner of sin or folly, of ignorance or unworthiness can remove us. Our life is hidden with Christ on high. We carry his nature, him the firstborn of many brothers and sisters, and every single member of the family bears his resemblance—even if we can't for the life of us see it ourselves.

We are our Beloved's, and our Beloved is ours. The Dove of the Beloved found a place to rest his foot and now brings all the life of creation and re-creation, making and remaking, the powers of binding and loosing, to each and to all of us.

For God, the whole body of Christ went into the waters and came up from the waters. The whole body of Christ receives the Spirit. The whole body of Christ is the beloved.

You. Me.

What does it mean to be the beloved? It means freedom and virtue and grace. It means possessing strength of spirit, moving in peace of heart. It means having eyes that do not think of mirrors as hateful things, having ears that can hear delight in oneself without screen or filter, having lips that can speak love without pretext or subtext. Love, given and received, unconditional.

But for all the joy that leaps in our hearts at hearing of such remarkable love, for all of our longing for this, it is foolishness to think that being the beloved of God is easy. In fact, Christ himself, the firstborn of us many brothers and sisters, foresaw that for all those who would follow him, belovedness would be anything but easy, anything but painless. He did promise, though, that the path of the beloved would lead to life.

Belovedness does not mean ease or comfort; it means strength and holiness. It does not mean the absence of suffering; it means the presence of love. Like the letter to the Hebrews states so beautifully, in speaking of our "birthright" as those made like Christ, Jesus learned obedience through the things that he suffered, and God disciplines all those he loves—so much so, that when the beloved ones suffer loss for Christ, they may understand that God is treating them like children. For whatever painful teachings may come, we can be confident they are

> for our good, in order that we may share his holiness. Now, discipline always seems painful rather than pleasant at the time, but later it yields the peaceful fruit of righteousness to those who have been trained by it. Therefore lift your drooping hands and strengthen your weak knees, and make straight paths for your feet, so that what is lame may not be put out of joint, but rather be healed. (Heb. 12:10–13)

This is a hard teaching that the Dove of heaven carries. Hard but good. Though the Father speaks full belovedness over us without condition or reservation, his love, rich and holy, burns like a consuming fire in us what is contrary to the nature of Jesus, lighting the way to walk his trail, difficult though it may be.

The Holy Spirit's love is like a ray, a beam, a single force, unop-posable and glorious, full of joy and power. Yet we perceive that same force differently depending on where we are, depending on what is inside us. If we are dark, we perceive his love as light; if we are hungry, we perceive it as food and nourishment; if we are broken, we perceive it as the setting of bones; if we are guilty, as forgiveness; if dead, we are brought to life, the very life of love, the very life of the Spirit who raised Christ from the dead like a grain of wheat.

BELOVEDNESS DOES NOT MEAN EASE OR COMFORT; IT MEANS STRENGTH AND HOLINESS. IT DOES NOT MEAN THE ABSENCE OF SUFFERING; IT MEANS THE PRESENCE OF LOVE.

The promise is that all of this is proof of belovedness—being utterly, lavishly provided for. There is no promise that that provi-sion will be easy or pleasant or will feel kind in the moment, only that it all must and shall be *agape*, unconditional love.

For some, belovedness means scourging and martyrdom. For others, it means honor and esteem. For all, though, belovedness is root and branch, fruit—and the flower before fruit. Life—not easy, but abundant and good. The very life of God in Christ, the Beloved. The very life of the Spirit, who, in spite of every difficulty, in spite of every action of opening and closing that might pain us, is called the Comforter.

Belovedness means death before new life, precisely what Jesus was implying when he said that for a man to save his life he must lose it first, or that by taking up our crosses, we might find the path that he walked. It is of this death, I think, that Henri Nouwen wrote in *Life of the Beloved*:

> Am I afraid to die? I am every time I let myself
> be seduced by the noisy voices of my world telling
> me that my "little life" is all I have and advising
> me to cling to it with all my might. But when I
> let these voices move to the background of my life
> and listen to that small soft voice calling me the
> Beloved, I know that there is nothing to fear and
> that dying is the greatest act of love, the act that
> leads me into the eternal embrace of my God whose
> love is everlasting.[5]

This eternal embrace, which for any pleasure, or any pain, has already begun for us in deep love, unconditional love witnessed and affirmed and delivered by the Holy Spirit. But if the heavens were to open above us now, would we be able to hear the voice of God?

Could we believe that we are truly the beloved?

We may never in this life see the heavens open above us. It could be that we never hear the voice of God, at least with the ears with which we hear most things. It could be that no dove alights on our head. But in faith, the inner truth of our reality is deeper than anything perceived with the senses. When God looks at you and me, he sees a daughter, a son. He sees the face of his own, his begotten and beloved Christ, who, as Hopkins said, "plays in ten thousand places, lovely in limbs, and lovely in eyes not his, to the Father through the features of men's faces."[6]

We are the beloved. The Spirit on us proves it.

What would it mean to live like it?

We would return to the love, the joy and pleasure of childhood, of the serious work of play and being. We would begin to live like God wants us to live, indeed, to live like God does.

Imagine.

THE WIND OF THE WILDERNESS
Journeying with the Spirit of the Desert

The Spirit immediately drove [Jesus] out into the wilderness.
He was in the wilderness forty days, tempted by Satan; and he
was with the wild beasts; and the angels waited on him.
—Mark 1:12–13

[I]n solitude our heart ... can grow so wide and
deep that nothing human is strange to it.
—Henri Nouwen, *Out of Solitude*

Let all teachers hold their peace; let all creatures be
silent in thy sight; speak unto me thou alone.
—Thomas à Kempis, *The Imitation of Christ*

If you are ever in Oregon, you must go some early morning on the eastern highway that runs beside the Columbia River down the floor of the great gorge between Portland and The Dalles. If the clouds are few, you will be greeted by a sunrise "lovely beyond any singing of it,"[1] clean and utterly strange, that washes and stripes the waterfalls and basalt columns with ageless, shifting color.

Travel toward the sun. When you see the signposts, turn off the highway and stop by the stone lodge flanking Multnomah Falls. You will see stairs that run up from the road, running past the lodge and to a lookout in view of the lower falls. At a particular point at the top of those stairs—count seven stones from the left at the top flight—stop, turn due west, and listen.

This is what you will hear: in your left ear, the roar of the massive two-tiered falls crashing interminably on themselves, foam on foam, the brisk yearlong snow melt dashing itself on black rocks that never dry. In your right ear, you will hear another roar—Interstate 84. Even in the blue morning it is loud, a ceaseless Doppler hum that whines and coughs and sends juvenile echoes up the ancient canyon. The thin rattle of a "crotch rocket" motorcycle, the clatter of a diesel rig shifting for the big turn, the whir of passenger cars bound east, bound west.

Two roars for two ears; the roar of nature and the roar of man.

Thinking on this, now climb the path that ascends to your right. The switchbacks aren't difficult, and the path is paved. Climb up to the stone bridge spanning the great lower pool, and mingle with the tourists—who are careful to keep a grip on their cameras. Most people stop here, but you are prepared for a hike, so you keep climbing. The trail turns steeper, sharper in turns, and more treacherous in footing. It climbs and keeps climbing.

You'll think that you've made it—you're at the top of the falls. But really, I don't want you stopping here at all. Keep hiking, south along the stream, deeper and deeper into the ancient forest. Listen to the sounds change, their timbre tempered by the soft cedars and sword ferns. The sorrel smells fresh when crushed and tastes like green apples when you chew it. In you go, in for hours, until you are hungry. You eat and keep walking. You drink and keep walking. Then at some point in the early afternoon, the trail veers away from the stream, away from the echoing gullies, and you are deep in the true backcountry, the soft, ancient stasis of the Hatfield Wilderness.

Now stop. Listen.

THE TRUE SILENCE OF THE SPIRIT IS PRESENCE AS MUCH AS IT IS ABSENCE. IT IS ENTERING A PLACE APART.

The two roars of this morning are miles away. You hear sounds, certainly—the forest is alive with them—but they are muted, hushed. Birdsong, mostly. Perhaps the tapping of a northern flicker seeking insects in the sloughing bark of a snag. The footfalls of small animals. The wind from the east. The thrum of flying ants.

When I have hiked into the true wilderness, it is the depth and quality of the silence that enters my soul and leaves me changed. When I meet people—and they are many—who say that their most profound encounters with God are in nature, it is this sense of quiet they usually want to remember. It is the sacred silence of a space, silent not because of the absence of sound, but silent because of the effect it has on the soul.

A holy silence of the interior, prompted by a sacred simplicity on the exterior.

A reminder that the true silence of the Spirit is presence as much as it is absence.

It is entering a place apart.

The year I graduated from seminary, my family packed our red station wagon in an August morning's predawn darkness and drove east on that highway past the falls. We were moving from Oregon to Illinois, to a new job, an apartment we'd leased sight unseen, and a whole portion of the United States we'd been content to fly over for our entire lives.

There are a good two thousand miles of mostly emptiness between Portland and Chicago. Navigating the long twilight stretches in between—from bright city to dim town to less-bright city to one-light desert rest stop—feels like one is a traveler among the stars: On a map one can see the constellations, but when you're traveling? You realize that most of the universe lies in the emptiness between.

We did not know, as we drove with the rising sun in our eyes every morning and the setting sun in our rearview mirror every night, what we would find when we arrived. We only felt that the move—to all appearances a quite risky one for our family—felt *right*. It was our path.

Both my wife and I, sitting as the green mileposts skipped by, had been in an inner desert for some time. In many ways the drive through the vast and lovely emptiness of the West became a metaphor for our great wilderness season. We had been in and out of it for a while. Hers is a story for her own book, but I, even while leading in churches, studying Greek and Hebrew until my eyes ached, and to all appearances a vibrant Christian, had been walking a wilderness I could barely recognize, let alone understand. I had become unsure of the contours of my own soul. In those years loved ones died, friends were lost, relationships were strained. In those years I sought myself until I despaired of the finding. Though never doubting the deepest foundation, I shook my faith down to bedrock until I felt that I had dismantled something and lost the manual for reassembly. My life became inordinately dark, darker than makes sense in writing of it, the darkness of space between the constellations.

Our first year in the Midwest was to be the pinnacle of this desert time, spiritually, relationally, and emotionally. We had left behind friends and homeland, the culture we were comfortable with, our favored activities. The leaving hurt as we drove, as the inner desert became an outer one. We shed tears.

My time in the spiritual desert lasted for years, a desolation with an occasional oasis. But that season was to be the most important time of my life. Forced by my surroundings to quiet myself, I began to embrace the silence. I did not know if or when it would end.

But I began to know the rough roar of silence as the voice of the Spirit. He was leading me, mysteriously, to a place apart.

I see now that it was very good.

If the Bible were a movie and if places were characters, "the wilderness" would hold a starring role. It's a recurring setting, all the way after the expulsion of humanity from the garden in Genesis, to the "wander in tears, forty years" of Israel's desert time, to the visions of Ezekiel, to the famous temptations of Christ, and Jesus's well-known habit of wandering into desert places for prayer.

The wilderness is a place of contradictions, a place portrayed in Scripture as an empty place yet full. The wilderness is cruel and bare, yet a setting for kindness and miraculous provision. The wilderness reveals things often by obscuring them. The wilderness welcomes God and the people of God by—sometimes concretely, sometimes abstractly—meeting evil.

More than anything, the wilderness is the background that most clearly highlights the high, good strangeness of the Holy Spirit, who, so often in Scripture, whistles like a wind among the rocks of the desert.

A cloud by day, a fire by night. Faithfully leading. Faithfully obscuring.

The Spirit's work in the life of his people is often a wild work, a desert work. He knows and loves the places that seem empty to us as much as he knows and loves the places that teem with life. He calls us to the wilderness to work in us in ways that could not be done well (perhaps not done at all) were we not drawn away, brought away, thrown away, finding ourselves on a lonely trail.

This was Jesus's experience. Directly after the soaring high of his baptism in the Jordan, the joy and affirmation of the Father speaking his belovedness over him, the Dove of heaven seemed to distend and whip apart into a lionlike whirlwind, launching Christ into the first great trial of his adult life. Here is Mark's account:

> Just as he was coming up out of the water, he saw the heavens torn apart and the Spirit descending like a dove on him. And a voice came from heaven, "You are my Son, the Beloved; with you I am well pleased."
>
> And the Spirit immediately drove him out into the wilderness. He was in the wilderness forty days, tempted by Satan; and he was with the wild beasts; and the angels waited on him (1:10–13).

The Greek word translated here as "drove out" is a rough one. It is βα'λλω (*balló*), from which we get our word *ball*, and as you would expect, it means to throw, fling, send flying, hurl.

It is not gentle.

Like a Major League Baseball pitcher sending a fastball straight through the strike zone, the Spirit in Mark's gospel downright hurls Jesus (the Beloved, remember) into the wilderness.

THE SPIRIT'S WORK IN THE LIFE OF HIS PEOPLE IS OFTEN A WILD WORK, A DESERT WORK.

The Spirit is not playing around. Nor is Jesus—who, in the more detailed accounts of this story elsewhere, is fasting, hungry and thirsty during this time in the desert. He is besieged with temptations in the wilderness—the temptation to work miracles on his own behalf rather than the Father's; the temptation for immediate acclamation and acceptance by the people who would eventually reject him, screaming for his crucifixion; and the temptation for an easy path to world power rather than the death-road, the God-road to the eternal kingdom promised to the seed of David.

All his suffering and all his overcoming are kept between the lines here in Mark. I like that. All that we are given here to make sense of Christ in the wilderness is the duration (the ancient "forty" of Noah's flood, of Moses on the mountain, of the wandering years of Israel in the desert), the Devil, the beasts, and the angels.

A long time. Danger, scarcity, abundance.

The wilderness.

And this, like every work of the Holy Spirit, was love.

Many long months after our eastward drive, I sat with my spiritual director, Father Stephen. Outside our church it was evening, one of those blue Illinois prairie evenings that betray those who call the Midwest ugly.

He asked me to describe my relationship with Jesus. I was silent for a minute, fumbling around inside my head until I came across the right words.

"It's as if," I began, "Jesus and I are sitting together in a dark room. He's not saying anything. I'm not saying anything. I look at him. He looks back at me. We're together. But silent. Quiet. Like we're each waiting for something."

He was quiet for a while himself. I sat, adjusted my chair. I wondered if I should continue to talk, to fill up the room between us with words. I didn't like the silence. I wanted to speak or for him to speak or for Jesus to speak. Anyone, really.

He breathed deeply.

"Silent?" he asked.

"Silent."

"Well, that's a very good place to start."

In her classic *Walking on Water*, Madeleine L'Engle wrote:

> When I am constantly running there is no time for
> being. When there is no time for being there is no
> time for listening. I will never understand the silent
> dying of the green pie-apple tree if I do not slow
> down and listen to what the Spirit is telling me, tell-
> ing me of the death of trees, the death of planets, of
> people, and what all these deaths mean in the light
> of the love of the Creator who brought them all into
> being; who brought me into being; and you.[2]

It's a beautiful truth, but a wilderness truth, a desert truth. A truth of windy silences—to somehow believe that to understand ourselves, to understand the great breath of creation, we must first walk backward, back along the trail, back through the deaths of things large and small, slowing life and heart and mind, all the while listening for the voice of God, all back, back, back, to the edge of the deep, to the starting place of being. That hazy place where the Spirit summons us up from the waters of beginning and whistles love and joy, creating and sustaining. "It's good that you are; how wonderful that you exist!"

We must know the Spirit's desert road, the trail away from the roars of man and nature. That kind of being is a difficult trick to master if we do not learn to know what silence—the real silence, of the soul, and not of the ears—sounds like. We must allow ourselves to learn it, perhaps *force* ourselves to learn it. Perhaps be forced to learn it, for our own good, to be forced to cease our running through thirst, exhaustion, danger, or simply the hollow dullness in our breasts that calls to us to seek refuge, to fly like a bird to our mountain.

It is time for the wilderness. Somehow, with the Spirit, we must learn to enter a place apart. For all its difficulty, it is a very good place to start.

The sacred silence of our interior becomes the void, the good and empty place into which the Spirit can speak. Like a kindly predator, he leads us into desert places—to separate us from the herd, to get at us alone, to approach from the flank, out of the sun, where our peripheral vision is hazy. He pounces, tumbles us in the sand and grit either roughly or gently. Away from the noise he carries or flings us, from the dullness of full belly and full brain. His beak sinks into bone and flesh, he tears us with blessings, tears us open sometimes till the red blood flows out so thick and abundant that we fear our life is leaving, that our bones will be left behind us when we wander on. And for all this, he makes no promises other than his love.

IF WE CAN BELIEVE IT, EVEN THE BITTEREST
WRESTLING WITH THE SPIRIT OUT IN
THE DESERT IS FOR OUR GOOD.

If we can believe it, even the bitterest wrestling with the Spirit out in the desert is for our good, the good of his beloved. We must sometimes suffer wounds before we can be bound again, better made and wiser than before, bearing the scars of wilderness as witnesses to the nearness of God.

This too is love, if we can accept it.

It is the wind of the wilderness, dry and cutting if necessary, that blows our own thoughts out of us and the Spirit's knowing into us. It is that wind that will eventually allow us to see though our eyes be closed and hear though our ears be deafened. It is the Holy Spirit, the wind of the wilderness, that flings us into the desert like rag dolls, cradles us out there like children, feeds us like the ravens above Elijah's creek. It is the wind that seeks to polish us with sand, to let the erosion of the grit reveal our truest contours. To see what we take with us out of nothing. What we leave with the nothing.

THE WILDERNESS IS WHERE THE SPIRIT TAKES OUR MASKS AWAY.

But for all this, who wishes for the wilderness? For some it has a romance before and after we are there and its own glass-like beauty that shimmers when we're in it, but for any beauty we may find, we still quail and quiver.

The wilderness is where the Spirit takes our masks away, where our own hearts are flayed, where the faces of devils and angels, once obscured by rocks and birds and lust and thirst, stare at us, challenging us to blink before they do. Sometimes he strips us naked and puts us in the dust, like Saul at the feet of Samuel.

The wind dries the eyes, dries them too rough and thin even to weep sometimes.

The wilderness can be a place that you walk to or a place inside of you or a place inside of another that you love. It can be death; it can be fasting. It can be loneliness, the loss of children conceived, the loss of children unconceived. It can be excruciating, obvious pain, or it can be dully, painfully ordinary—a struggle so "meaningless" you blush to even share it.

And it is usually walked alone.

HE ONLY PROMISES LOVE. NO ANSWERS. NOT EASE.

So what are we to make of a Spirit—the Spirit of the same Jesus who knew the pain of wilderness so well—who not only *accompanies* us into the desert but *throws* us into it? If it is true that he is the wind at our back, blowing us into places abandoned by men, places hard to live in and dry, places of thorn and curse and cruelty, places of the sun by day and the catamount or wild dogs by night, then what are we to say to him for such treatment? "Thank you"?

I mean no presumption, and I speak this in faith. If we cannot say thank you for the desert yet, then it is likely because we are still in it. The wind of the wilderness, ever seeking your good, does not expect your gratitude when you have not eaten for forty days.

"What are you doing here?" The ancient question hangs, as it did for Elijah, over the mountain, over the hot bedrock of the desert. But we might as well ask it of the Asker. And who knows if we will receive an answer that human ears can understand?

He only promises love. No answers. Not ease.

Only love.

The true terror of the desert is the terror of scarcity, the terror of absences. These are the slow fears—the emptying canteen; the disappearing food rations; the absence of shelter, shade, water, human kindness, life itself.

But the true promise of the desert, or of any wilderness, literal or metaphorical, is found in the presences whose existence would be impossible to know without such absences. We cannot know the clarifying presence of a fast until the absence of food. We cannot know the depth of the white-blue days or the starry nights until the absence of a roof. We cannot know the richness of silence until the absence of sound. Abundance, for humans at least, is usually invisible except when scarcity is in the foreground. The difference in the end is all in the seeing.

There is something that awakens inside the soul when one realizes that in God's view of the world there is no such thing as scarcity.

Let me tell you one of my favorite stories of abundance. I will try to tell it as it was told to me by my friend Randy, a Keetoowah Cherokee:

In the 1950s, Canada's government was consolidating rule in the Arctic by forcing the native Inuit peoples onto settlement reservations. One old man, a grandfather, resisted. He did not want to live in the white peoples' houses. He did not want to eat their food. He did not want to lose his culture.

His family, concerned that he might do something rash in his yearning for the old freedom, took away his weapons, his tools, his precious knife—all that he needed to live off the land in the frozen, blustery tundra.

Or at least they thought they took everything away. They could not take away his knowledge, his way of seeing things. And his way of seeing was the most important thing he had.

One dark night, as the wind shrieked around his place, the grandfather stepped out into the blizzard. He was empty-handed, but only for a moment. He defecated into his hand, molding his own "waste" into a keen blade as it froze, spitting on it, wetting and sharpening the bloodletting side with saliva. It froze solid and sharp. He took the knife and killed a dying dog, skinning it to make coat and harness. He used its rib cage for a sled, its flesh for food. He hitched up a healthy dog, and with a flourish of his blade, the grandfather disappeared into the white desert.

The grandfather was strong in the old ways of seeing things—that is to say, seeing the world, for all its dangers, as a place (in its own desolate way) of abundance.

For all appearances to the contrary, there is no such thing as scarcity where the Spirit is concerned, even in the wilderness, even after the forty-day fast. The bare clarity of the desert may corner us, reduce us, winnow us, take us next door to death, even, but if the process is allowed to work, we will see, gradually or all of a sudden, that we have never been alone, that there has never been utter silence, that tools and food and fire and comfort and meaning and the kindness of God can be everywhere, even here, for those who can see things as the Spirit sees them.

Abundance can be found in the desert or tundra, in the ancient woods of the Hatfield wilderness, in barren and swarming Chicago. Abundance can look like barely enough sometimes, sometimes like scarcity itself—five loaves and two fish before a hungering multitude. Abundance is not defined by our tastes, our prayers, our desires, or our demands. Abundance is the simple reality.

After all, in spite of the hunger and thirst, who, among all those whom God led into the wilderness, starved there? Who died of thirst?

For the wind of the wilderness, there is no such thing as scarcity, no such thing as emptiness. In spite of any curse and harshness, even the desert places whisper back the "very good" to their Maker, who rustles the sage and dances among the rattlesnakes.

The difference of the desert is the difference of the *seeing*. If we think the Spirit is cruel to blow us into the windy and desolate places, then we have not yet understood this. We need such barrenness much more than we think.

As I said, something good snaps inside the mind when we realize that abundance is everywhere.

What? Is that not what I said?

The wind of the wilderness blows where it wishes. The Spirit's presence can be as arid and contradictory as the desert—but always in the service of love.

Where he blows, cities can dry up around you, families, and neighbors, and friends, and everything be blown into hollow husks for a time. But the one who calls us is ever faithful, and though he promises nothing but love (even our deaths are possible in the deserts where he leads us), that promise is as sure as the very nature of God.

At some point, every person's path leads into the wilderness. Into the desert, to be quiet for a time, or perhaps to rage and to curse God where only ravens and silent angels can hear. Sometimes we wander there; sometimes we walk with purpose. We look for the path. Sometimes it is clear. At other times the sands cover even our own footprints. Sometimes it is a place emptier than empty; sometimes we glimpse a silhouette under the cleft of a rock or a cloaked figure moving parallel to us down a far ravine. The wilderness is empty of words; it is full of meaning. It is silent yet howls until the head pounds. Sometimes it is an experience of such profound suffering that others wonder how you make it. Sometimes it is so simple and personal that others wonder why you don't just "get over it."

In any case, being thrown into the wilderness is an act of love. There are no promises whether you will live or die. But even there, in the deepest desert, the Spirit can lead you to wells of living water.

When I meet people who say that their most profound encounters with God are in nature, I sometimes laugh. Nature is not just a lovely sunset; it is dull fog, sleet, bitter muck. It is not just the waterfall; it is the drought. It is not just the green flourishing; it is the brown and red deaths, the white sickness, the black of mold and decay.

AT SOME POINT, EVERY PERSON'S PATH LEADS INTO THE WILDERNESS.

I laugh not because their sentiment is untrue. Because it *is* true. The desert, like all places, is the dwelling of the Holy Spirit. Presence in absence. And though he may cast you there, he will fling himself alongside you, rough as sackcloth, gray as ashes, and good. He does that so that in the emptiness, like so many before us (like Jesus himself), we might find fullness; in the absence, presence; in the scarcity, abundance; in fasting, a feast spread in the presence of our enemies.

In the roar of the wind in both ears, the joyous shriek of the Dove of creation, that ghostly white wind of the wilderness, you might hear him asking the ancient question: *What are you doing here?*

He knows your answer already, but it is no matter: you have been kindly hunted, brought or carried or thrown here because it is you who must answer it.

What you say may determine your life.

THE BIRTH FROM ABOVE

Growing with the Spirit of New Life

We are inflamed, by Thy Gift we are kindled; and are carried upwards.
—Augustine of Hippo, *Confessions*

*For if we see that the sun, in sending forth its rays upon the earth,
to generate, cherish, and invigorate its offspring, in a manner
transfuses its substance into it, why should the radiance of the Spirit
be less in conveying to us the communion of his flesh and blood?*
—John Calvin, *Institutes of the Christian Religion*

*Very truly, I tell you, no one can see the kingdom of God without
being born from above.... I tell you, no one can enter the kingdom
of God without being born of water and Spirit. What is born
of the flesh is flesh, and what is born of the Spirit is spirit. Do
not be astonished.... The wind blows where it chooses, and you
hear the sound of it, but you do not know where it comes from or
where it goes. So it is with everyone who is born of the Spirit.*
—John 3:3, 5–8

I stood on the banks of the Jordan River, under the trees of Yardenit, where pilgrims come to wash and pray. In the brown water swam

innumerable catfish, as big around as my leg and as bold as unwel-
come dogs. They lazed in the weeds of the undercut banks, mouthed
at unseeable morsels, rolled their white bellies sunward in the slow
current.

Other white bellies turned sunward too: the pale robes of the
pilgrims, come here from all corners of the world to be baptized in
water that had touched the flesh of the Man from Nazareth. They
were beautiful in their awkward enterings into the water—great
barrel-chested Russians and Ukrainians, aged pilgrims from Korea,
Americans in all states of sunburn and foreign naïveté, dark and
lovely Africans doffing bright shirts and dresses for the sheer robes
of baptism. Carloads and busloads of people, old and young people,
skins-of-every-shade people, blue-eyed and brown- and green- and
black-eyed people.

There at the banks of Christ's waters, the first and last waters, the
face of the deep, all status and form and nationality fell aside in favor
of flimsy white cloth, cloth that sank with them, then clung to limbs
and shoulders like a new skin as they broke back into the sun—some
once, some thrice, some seven times going beneath and above the
water, like fresh-faced second infants.

The human form takes on instinctive grace in the water.
Something awakens when the body slips into the sea or the pool of a
deep stream, an unconscious ancient life that makes us relax, smile,
fan our arms like lean wings under the rippling surface, hinting at
why some scientists call our race "aquatic apes," a term that human-
izes rather than demeans. I think of this every time I see a swimmer.

Watch! The dive from above, as confident and daring in its own
way as any arboreal ape's elegant swing to a new limb, elemental and

direct, piercing, instinctive. Animal in the most human way imaginable. The water is laid open. The swimmer hangs for a second under the splash. Limbs contract, then kick out, strong, raising silt and pebbles from below. The arching reach from the shoulders, beautifully simian, as thumbs and fingers, gently webbed at their bases, curve from elongated arms under the surface.

WE ARE CREATURES OF THE HERE AND THERE, OF THE BEACHES AND SHORES, OF ALL THE BORDERLAND PLACES.

Going to the water is like going to a childhood home, at once sweet and fearful. It is surely beautiful, full of conscious and unconscious remembrance. It is also heavy with the knowledge that it's a nice place to visit now, but you wouldn't want to live there.

We are creatures of the here and there, of the beaches and shores, of all the borderland places that I have already told you I love. Seen in the life of the Spirit, in our very nature we embody tensions, paradoxes of birth.

Screwtape (C. S. Lewis's literary demon) calls humans "amphibians—half spirit and half animal." "A revolting hybrid," he comments, disgusted by God's making of our race as a bridge between different ways of being.[1] We humans unite, as it were, the sea and the earth, the earth and the sky, the sky and the void of space, the void and whatever happy country lies beyond it. We are border crossers, pilgrims belonging to many countries, mobile souls. We have been given both the seen and unseen as our natural habitat, the sea and the dry land. We flourish or fail as individuals based on how well we bridge our various dwelling places, whether we gracefully pull off the upward dives.

I stood watching bodies move in the water. The Jordan is not wide; at Yardenit it is narrow enough to throw a pop can across to a friend, who would not catch foam when she opened it. The banks are lined with eucalyptus. If you move far enough back from the tree line, you can see Galilee, and beyond, the studded hills of the Golan Heights.

I had driven with my group down from the Heights earlier that day. We were a small press trip visiting Israel and Palestine—a few Protestants, a Roman Catholic, and our guides. Starting in Tiberias that morning, we had driven up perhaps three thousand feet into the hills, along fanatically curved roads—still part of the DMZ where the marks of old battles and warnings of minefields still mingle starkly with the farms and fences of the fertile land. Our guide, a veteran of the 1967 war, spoke as we drove and stopped—spoke of war with one's neighbors, what it had been like to lead young men into skirmishes from which they did not return, of how it felt to shoot a man when you could see his eyes, of the time it had taken him to heal from it afterward.

The Heights, still hotly contested between Syria and Israel, are a study in contrast and conflict. Farms and gardens grow on former military stations, the remnants of still-recent war forming concrete backdrops to orchards, pastureland, and rolling gardens. From one place near apple trees, we could see far enough into Syria to make out villages where their civil war still raged. Our guide laughed darkly when he talked about it and encouraged us to keep moving—stray rockets are quite rare, but occasionally they land among the *kibbutzim*.

I rode shotgun for our trip, perhaps because I was the youngest of our group, perhaps because I did not mind that our driver smelled of endless cigarettes. On this stretch of road, I was particularly grateful for the front seat. The natural beauty of the Heights is striking, one of the only places in Israel where the land is dramatically formed by basalt, the remnant of volcanic action. The rocky crags are softened by green, Mount Hermon to the north carries snow, and the whole land has the lush strangeness of gardens in a desert. It is a place where cacti flower alongside apples.

But there were other glimpses too—of places where men had died, borderland ground that knew the flicker of small arms and the shushing lullaby of rockets. We drove the morning away, through sunshine and orchards, past thorny cacti and barbed wire, fences for cattle and fences for men—rigged to scramble nearby troops should their electric current be broken.

Driving past a rocketed bunker, we struck a white bird, killing it against our windshield. Its blood and the dusty mark of a splayed wing was in front of me until we reached Jerusalem.

But then down we drove, windows down, eyes down, through the brown switchbacks, down into sight of Galilee, down to the reeds and rushes and pilgrims that wash and pray and dress in white down along the yellow Jordan at Yardenit.

Down to touch the water.

Of the four gospels, the one that the beloved John wrote is something special. John speaks the language of my heart. He wrote later in
his life than the other evangelists, and you can tell it from his prose,
his style, his spiritual obsessions—he is much more interested in the
whys of Christ than the *whats*.

Carried by the Spirit, John wrote at that rarest human moment,
when a person's old age flashes into the brightest clarity of life, like
the precious nub of a candle that somehow illuminates a whole room
before sputtering out. The gospel of John is the brilliance of a sharp
old man in the second wind of his second childhood.

For old-young John, everything in the universe was part of a
duality. Above and below. Light and darkness. The now and the yet
to come. The liar and the truth teller, the seeing and the blind, the
lover and the hater, the hidden and the revealed. The Christ, the
Antichrist. There is a spare mathematic to his theology, all powers
of two. His equations often elude me, but I instantly see they are
balanced.

In John's theology, divisions—of time, space, holiness, illumination—are stark. But Christ crosses them. Jesus the Word moves from
heaven to earth; brings us from darkness to light; bridges the now
with the soon-to-come; reveals what is hidden; brings seeing to the
blind, truth to liars, piercing the veil between old and new.

The ancient symbol of John and his gospel is the eagle, strong
and clear-sighted, remarkable for making its home in the great empty

middle, halfway between above and below, part of them both, solely belonging to neither. It fits.

At the table of Christ's Last Supper, John reclined against the Teacher. In the gospel he wrote as an old man, he recounted what had happened immediately before:

> Jesus, knowing that the Father had given all things into his hands, and that he had come from God and was going to God, got up from the table, took off his outer robe, and tied a towel around himself. Then he poured water into a basin and began to wash the disciples' feet and to wipe them with the towel that was tied around him. He came to Simon Peter, who said to him, "Lord, are you going to wash my feet?" Jesus answered, "You do not know now what I am doing, but later you will understand."
> (John 13:3–7)

Later we would understand.

Through water, Jesus was upending the world, replacing every broken understanding of masters and servants, of high and low, of above and below, replacing them with the truth. He, the firstborn through the Holy Spirit of God's new humanity, was a bridge, a border crosser, the one who could go through water and come out of water, and call up out of water a new creation.

The whole scene there in the upper room in Jerusalem was beautiful, intimate. As the bread ("my body, which is given for you," Luke 22:19) and wine ("the new covenant in my blood," Luke 22:20) circled the table, beginning a meal that has never ceased, John, the beloved disciple, leaned back against Jesus. He heard the heart of God pumping blood in the chest of a laborer from a village in the northern hills. He heard Christ's breath rustle like feathers in his lungs, perhaps sensed his pulse and breathing quicken, his throat tighten when Judas rose and left the table into the night.

I wonder how many times he thought of those words, as an old man, an exile, waiting for the death and new life that he had heard and seen and written of so starkly.

"Later you will understand."

I remember the moment I was born. Not the first time, but the second.

I think it was on the Fourth of July that followed my seventh birthday. I remember being young, my new-believer parents having introduced me to Sunday school a few months before. I knelt by my wooden bed in the hot summer upstairs of our old farmhouse, and in words that I do not at all remember, simply said *yes* to God. And by faith, I was born anew, born again, born from above.

Here is the miracle of the thing: any observer would only have seen a freckle-nosed boy murmuring by a pillow—no angels descending, no dove alighting, no voice from heaven. But of all the moments in my life, this was one of the very most significant. I hesitate to say that this is the moment when I was *saved*, because I feel that every day between that one and this has been a tiny step in the process of Christ-likening. But I have no doubt at all that this was the moment I was *born*. That mystical minute, I believe, saw little me dive with a child's faith from death to life, from emptiness to abundance, from small darkness into expansive light. That moment was one of happy hope, a feeling of indescribable lightness, a sense that if it was bidden, my heart could fly.

Later I would understand.

A couple of years later, my father would baptize me, on the birthday of my little brother Christian (who died a year before, when he was three days old). I was less than ten. A child. But my immaturity did not keep me from wholeheartedly affirming the life of the Father, Son, and Holy Spirit as *my* life, and as I went down into the warm water and was pulled up again, my own white robe sticking to my bones, I felt the flutterings of the Holy One against my ribs. I knew I was beloved.

The decades since then have been a long growing up. Like any newborn creature, my spiritual self went through infancy, childhood, and adolescence. I had growth spurts and reversions to earlier stages of development. Various seasons brought doubts, transgressions, frustrations, darknesses, and second darknesses. I experienced farm and forest, desert and oasis, rough and bitter struggle and great flourishing joy.

But in all of it, even at the most difficult turns of the trail, I never doubted one thing. I was alive. I had been born by the Spirit.

John's nearly mad commitment to the dualities of the world brings magnificent power to his account of Jesus's famous meeting with Nicodemus. Their conversation in John 3 is one of the best-known passages of the Bible, perhaps one of the best-known of all literature.

It is dark when Nicodemus, the good Pharisee, comes to Christ, the dangerous rabbi. "Rabbi," he says, "we know that you are a teacher who has come from God; for no one can do these signs that you do apart from the presence of God" (v. 2).

To such a sincere compliment, spoken from such an unlikely source, any well-adjusted person would say a polite thank-you or perhaps would inquire of the new seeker's story to attempt some pleasant evening conversation. Jesus, though, is far more than a well-adjusted person.

)) (

GOD IS DOING A NEW THING.

The one who taught with authority abruptly wrests the conversation from the safer teacher of Israel, changing the subject so fast as to cause whiplash. Jesus answers him, "Very truly, I tell you, no one can see the kingdom of God without being born from above" (v. 3).

Snap.

You can almost hear the silence for a minute or two, Nicodemus pondering where the conversation will go from here, struggling to understand, wanting to understand the new rabbi's teaching, the meaning eluding him. Capturing his confusion, "born from above" is a play on words in the original Greek of John's book—the same phrase can be translated "born again." Both senses play in the context here, as understandings and misunderstandings tangle with the foundational truth of the cosmos, and Nicodemus is strung between them like a tightrope walker in sandals.

He moves to the literal, asking Jesus delicately if, *ahem*, a man can, you know, *go back in?* Christ, ever compassionate, does not answer that one directly, but explains the reproductive process of the kingdom of heaven—that in the same way that flesh bears flesh, fruit after its kind, so the Spirit bears spirit. This reproduction is like wind, Jesus says, unpredictable, perceivable chiefly by its effects, and from above.

God is doing a new thing.

Nicodemus is incredulous. Later he would understand.

Medieval alchemists thought a lot like John—in pairs, dualities, flashes of symbolic logic that both did and did not belong to the world that everyday people live in. They had a saying, attributed to the mythical magician Hermes Trismegistus—"as above, so below."[2] It referred to the magical or alchemical belief that in some mysterious manner, the macrocosm (the whole, the above, the general, the universe) was intimately twined with the microcosm (the part, the below, the specific, me and you).

As the centuries rolled on, this perceived principle was extrapolated into a hundred varieties of quackery and deception (every so often bearing some accidental fruit of wisdom), including various permutations of the Zodiac, conflicting systems of sympathetic magic, and in general the overarching idea that throughout the cosmos the big and the little somehow share a linked destiny.

This, of course, was mostly nonsense by the time it resulted in, say, an attempted recipe to produce gold from lead. But like most nonsense, a seed of truth was buried underneath a few dozen layers of husk, a truth so close to us that we have largely forgotten it.

THE LABOR PAINS OF CREATION, THE WHOLE WORLD AFFECTED BY THE FALL OF MAN, ARE NOT PERMANENT.

The truth is this: that the redemption of each of us individuals by the Holy Spirit, the "birth from above," the giving of the new nature, the heavenly method of reproduction, is *scalable*. What does this mean? That the redemption of the fallen order of the sin-stained cosmos mirrors the redemption of each and any of us who is born of the Spirit.

The apostle Paul, in his letter to the church in Rome, wrote:

> The creation waits with eager longing for the
> revealing of the children of God … in hope that
> the creation itself will be set free from its bondage
> to decay and will obtain the freedom of the glory of
> the children of God. We know that the whole cre-
> ation has been groaning in labor pains until now;

and not only the creation, but we ourselves, who
have the first fruits of the Spirit, groan inwardly
while we wait for adoption, the redemption of our
bodies. (Rom. 8:19–23)

Paul's vision is as big as the world. The labor pains of creation,
the whole world affected by the fall of man, are not permanent. In
fact, the suffering and current bentness of the very created order
echo those pains that every one of us who has been born from
above feels in ourselves. Paul thinks that this second Spirit birth, as
potent as it may be, is only the firstfruits, a sample, the merest taste
of what will come at the full renewing, when we and Nicodemus
and John and the soil, the water, the air, the grasshopper and praying mantis, the crested Steller's jay, the iridescent rainbow trout,
the white oaks, the western red cedars, the whole, the above, the
general, the universe mirrors the very redemption applied to our
lives by the Holy Spirit of the divine Trinity that is even now being
born in us by the new nature.

This is the upside-down reproductive process of heaven, the
life of God in Christ through the Holy Spirit growing to fill and
redeem the totality of creation.

And that promise of the coming birth is in us as surely as the
second birth has made us new, as surely as the Spirit rests in and
on and with and above us, like a grand nesting bird, brooding
over us little microcosms as once he did over the whole, as indeed
he is doing now while waiting for the hatch. It is very strange and
very good.

To twist the old magic: "As below, so above."

At strange sacred moments in our lives, we hang motionless, neither here nor there. These are the moments of bridge crossing, of border crossing, of listening to bells chime midnight, the nowhere place between the days. These are the moments we stand in crossroads in the moonlight, the moment between laying our head on our beloved and hearing his or her heartbeat, the moment between the altar and the honeymoon suite, between a mother's labor and the baby's birth, between planting wildflowers and seeing the first sprout. This is the white moment when the pilgrim closes her eyes and descends into the Jordan, long hair lazing downstream.

The whole world lives in this moment, the groaning before the new life, the slow changing of us. The promise that the cosmos is being healed, born from above by the power of God.

This is the moment when the boy kneeling at the bed says *yes* to a God he can love but cannot understand, *yes* to a path of discipleship at once more grim and more life giving than anything he can yet imagine. This is the moment his earthly father lowers him into the water with love in his eyes. This is still the moment, years later, when he doubts all he knows besides the reality of the life God promises to the dead. The moment he will live in for the rest of his life, all a nurturing of the infant life of Jesus in the secret place in his soul. This is the moment of mystery—the moment of the birth from above—the moment of the Spirit.

This is now.

Some say that the first generations of Christians were baptized naked, a symbol of the true new birth, of the rich poverty of the new nature, the return to the state of holy Eden, and the family-ness of the community of faith. The tradition ended quickly, though—the pastoral implications of a congregation who had all seen each other naked proved to be too much to handle (I assume that both lust and its opposite were motivating factors), and the false rumors among outsiders about the "orgies" that this foolish cult of slaves and misfits held around their sacred octagonal pools wasn't helping the Christian reputation among more respectable pagans.

I don't think that we should reinstate the practice, but did we not lose something beautiful when it went away? In a world where we all still hide our nakedness yet long to be newborn, new-seen, new-known, do we not all long with a longing far deeper than simply for sex for others to see us as we truly are and still accept us as their own? Do we not long to be seen naked and unashamed? Doesn't the naked welcome carry more power and mystery than the clothed? Don't we know by some inner-ear instinct of the heart that water should strip away everything? It is a return, a dive upward, a home-coming for new creations.

What would it mean if every drop of water was the waters of creation? What would it mean if you and I who are "being saved" were redeemed the way the world is being redeemed—by inches, not miles, but at the same time, all at once? What if you and the universe shared a common story line?

If any of this is true, then it is the Spirit's work, sure as breathing. It sure seems like something he would do.

In the great story of the Bible, the real birth events are invariably accompanied by water and the Spirit. The Spirit hovering over the waters of the black deep. The dove sent by Noah over the waters of the flood. The birth of Israel—a wind that parted the waters of the Red Sea, making a road where there was no road and delivering a new people bound for a new land. The images and tools of that people's tabernacle and temple—the brass sea, the seven-branched lampstand that illuminated the way to the Holy of Holies.

THE WHOLE WORLD LIVES IN THIS MOMENT, THE GROANING BEFORE THE NEW LIFE, THE SLOW CHANGING OF US. THE PROMISE THAT THE COSMOS IS BEING HEALED, BORN FROM ABOVE.

Think of Elijah's drenched altar at the turning of the tide of Israel's religious unfaithfulness—three times he commanded water to be poured on it, and still the fire of heaven fell to delight in the sacrifice and show that it was accepted. Remember the Spirit who hovered above the woman Mary's waters. On her words, "Let it be with me according to your word" (Luke 1:38), the inner spark was kindled, in spite of every rule of logic. Call to mind the words of John the Baptizer that the one who was to come would use fire itself as if it were water, a thing to baptize in. Recall also Jesus's baptism, the founding and consecration of a new deliverance—the Dove descended that day over the muddy Jordan. Think of the lamplit conversation with the Pharisee

Nicodemus—Christ's playful double entendre: "No one can enter the kingdom of God without being born of water and Spirit" (John 3:5).

"Born of water and the Spirit," Jesus said. And that pairing provides an intricate web of theme and symbol throughout John's gospel, his largest epistle, and the book of Revelation. John's books are sopping with holy water, symbolizing life, cleansing, renewal, and the abundance of the Spirit.

Christ in John is a Christ of the waters—Jesus's first miracle at Cana (at a wedding feast, he turns vats of ritual water into knock-your-sandals-off, top-shelf wine), his famous conversation under the stars with Nicodemus, his conversation at the well with the woman who came to draw water and left thinking of the Spirit, his cure of the lame man at the pool of Bethesda (where an angel troubled the impossible, healing waters), his journeys across the sea of Galilee, his walking on the whitecapped water of the same sea in the middle of a storm, his strange teaching that a spring of living water will gush from those who live his life, the healing of the blind man, where he spat water into the clay, pressed it to dead eyes, and told the man to wash them clean in a pool.

Remember how the salt water fell from the face of Jesus when he wept at the grave of his dead friend Lazarus, how Christ stripped naked on the night he was betrayed, and, wrapped only in a towel, washed the feet of those who had walked so far with him. Then think of the water that poured out of his pierced side, mingled with blood. The tears of Mary, too, on finding the tomb of her Teacher (she thought) desecrated. And recall Christ, revealed the third time after his resurrection, walking by the Sea of Tiberias, a vision so strange and lovely that Peter dove into the sea, not believing that a boat could make it to shore faster than his body.

On the shore of the sea, the one who died and yet lives cooked fish for breakfast over a fire of gathered sticks. He fed his friends. In the lulls of their conversation, they heard the water, the slap of waves against the shore.

Before his ascension into heaven, Christ taught us and sent us to spread the news and power of this birth from above. What had been created was now being re-created, what had been born once of water would now be twice born, of the Spirit as well as nature, in the open secret of the re-creation of all things.

So we who follow the God-man go, into and among every people in every place in every time for the rest of history. We teach and we baptize, carrying water and walking in the Spirit, preaching that the kingdom has come, now among all those who have been born twice, and soon to come to the entire groaning world.

PRAISE THE SPIRIT OF LIFE UNDER
THE FACE OF THE REDEEMING DEEP,
PRAISE HIM BELOW, PRAISE HIM ABOVE,
PRAISE HIM IN EVERY MIDDLE PLACE.

The water we baptize with is the ancient water, ever fresh, sanctified and sanctifying by the power of the Spirit who still rustles its surface. This is the reproductive process of heaven. Dive upward into the water, breaking the surface with animal grace, the long reach into your deepest eternal habitat. Feel the joy of homecoming, whatever groans may persist. Praise the Spirit of life under the face of the redeeming deep, praise him below, praise him above, praise him in every middle place.

This is the splash.

This is the pilgrim moment.

This is the life.

THE FLAME OF PURE SPEECH
Understanding the Spirit Who Speaks

We keep the feast of Pentecost,
and the Spirit's sojourning,
and the appointed day of promise,
and the fulfillment of our hope,
and the mystery so great,
so mighty and so reverend.
Wherefore, unto Thee we cry:
Creator of the world, Glory to Thee.
—From the Eastern liturgy for Pentecost Sunday

Suddenly from heaven there came a sound like the rush of a violent
wind, and it filled the entire house where they were sitting. Divided
tongues, as of fire, appeared among them, and a tongue rested on
each of them. All of them were filled with the Holy Spirit and
began to speak in other languages, as the Spirit gave them ability.
—Acts 2:2–4

My hotel room's little corner window looked out on a crooked alley in the heart of Jerusalem, where green rebel vegetation pushed its way through the edges of the pavement. I'd slept with the window partly open. I woke slowly to the sun slanting into the room, the arid smells of Palestine, and the sounds of a waking city. Traffic droned a street or two away, someone up the alley called *Achi!* (My brother!), with a laughing response from a second voice I couldn't understand. Under it all was the hiss of spring rain. I washed, dressed, and walked downstairs. I was in Jerusalem for Pentecost.

I descended into a celebration that had woken up long before I did. The first floor was almost literally a zoo. In the courtyard of my upscale hotel, goats and sheep and all sorts of hairy things were huddled into corners, bleating and chewing at great bundles of produce, symbols of plenty heaped among upturned baskets. Greenery everywhere. Children—swarms of children—surrounded the animals, capering through the lobby, leaping in front of bellhops, making faces at me (I returned the favor), clambering on tables and sculptures and strangers and great-grand-strangers. Their parents and siblings and guardians and victims pursued them, halfheartedly chiding in a dozen languages, balancing espressos.

They were Jews from the world over, gathered in Jerusalem according to their families for *Shavuot*, the Feast of Weeks, Pentecost. There were Jews from Brooklyn and Argentina and Brazil, Jews from Europe, Western and Eastern, Jews from the long beaches of Los Angeles and Haifa. Abraham's kids from the whole world over. Their shared heritage, their cultural story called to them from beyond the borders of nation-state or hemisphere to this little golden city, tucked out of the way behind the ear of the world.

A happily barbarian Gentile like me felt like a wallflower, planted at the edge of a dance that started centuries before my language began to be spoken.

This was happy chaos, the chaos of harvest, of gathering.

The Pentecost I saw was not that different from its much more famous ancestor two thousand years earlier.

Jews from across the known world gathered in Jerusalem for the festival seven weeks after Christ's passion. Scattered from centuries of exile across the Roman world and bringing along many of the prose-lytes who worshipped the unseen God of Israel, they came to celebrate the great spring festival commanded in the teaching of Moses, came here to the mountain of Jerusalem to worship, in sight of the temple and the City of David.

The dispersion, *diaspora*, of these Jews from the land of Israel to the nations is painful cultural history—a history of scattering against their will, of falling from the glory of the days of David and Solomon to being a conquered people, a reenslaved people by Assyrian and cruel Babylonian, by Median and Persian and Roman. Tribes united by blood were torn apart into exile and tossed into the muddy babble and confusion of the Gentile world. They wondered even how to worship when severed from their homeland.

The painful reminders of that exile would have been all around them—a despised tax collector working for the haughty Romans, the palaces of Pilate the governor and Herod the puppet-king, Roman legionnaires in the streets with their swords sheathed at the hip, soldiers who catcalled the women and made old men carry their packs. The money used to buy lodging and food for the festival bore the head of Caesar, exchanged between hands that thought graven images idolatry.

The gathering travelers that Pentecost day heard whispered stories of an execution only seven weeks before they got into town, the killing of an itinerant rabbi from the hill country who did not contest the matter when he was called *meshiach*, the Messiah, the Anointed One. Only as long ago as Passover, the priests had convinced the Romans to execute the teacher publicly, in a manner most cruel and cursed. But his body, some said, in spite of the guard and public seals placed over his corpse, had not stayed in the grave.

He had been seen by the sea.

PENTECOST WAS A FIRSTFRUITS PARTY.

Pentecost was the joy of coming home and the knowledge that it was home no longer. A joy and a pain for the gathering Jews of the world. A time to remember their unique unity that could keep tradition and tongue alive even though planted in the bitterest soils, but also to mourn the scattering that God had allowed because of the ancient sins of their fathers and mothers.

Pentecost was a firstfruits party, a celebration for the Jews in the streets outside the home of Christ's friends. But not all of the bounty brought in was pleasant to taste. There were some bitter grapes among the crop, and the children's teeth were set on edge.

They longed to taste something different, something just beyond what words could describe.

This was the day the Spirit would fall in a new way.

Do you remember the Tower of Babel?

On an ancient plain called Shinar, the story goes, the people of the earth banded together for a great project. Genesis 11 talks about it. Here's the account in my translation from the original Hebrew:

All the earth had one tongue, one speech. And it so happened, during their journeying from the east, they found a plain in the land of Shinar and lived there. Each man said to his friend, "Come—let us make bricks with fire, and bake them well." Bricks were stones for them, and tar was mortar. Then they said, "Come—let us build a city for ourselves, and a tower whose head is in the heavens. Let us make a name for ourselves, so that we will not be scattered over the face of the whole world."

The LORD came down to see the city and tower built by the sons of Adam. He said, "Look—one people, with one tongue—and all of this is just the beginning of their doings. Nothing will be impossible for them. They will do whatever they plan. Come, let us go down and mix their tongue, so that no man may hear his friend."

In this way, the LORD scattered them from there, scattered them over the face of all the earth, and they ceased building the city.

Because of this, it was named Babel.

At first glance it is a strange story. Many cultures have an origin-of-languages tale, and many more have the actions of a capricious god, but for the God of Israel to seemingly feel threatened by a tower built from tar and baked mud? Not particularly awe-inspiring.

At second glance it becomes a stranger story. After all, the humans in the story are striving for unity, are they not? Unity is good. Right? They seek to make culture, to build, to cooperate, to unite for craftsmanship, for togetherness. God descends, seeming like the ultimate party pooper, not only ending the project but ending the possibility of all future projects like it, taking away the glorious ability for all of humanity to speak and be understood.

But at third glance, what do you see?

The beginning of a stranger story still.

The beginning of a Spirit story.

Let's fly forward through the centuries, to another city, to another gathering, to another great project with the heavens as its aim. Luke recorded the story in the second chapter of the book of Acts:

> When the day of Pentecost had come, they were all together in one place. And suddenly from heaven there came a sound like the rush of a violent wind, and it filled the entire house where they were sitting. Divided tongues, as of fire, appeared among them, and a tongue rested on each of them. All of

them were filled with the Holy Spirit and began
to speak in other languages, as the Spirit gave
them ability.

Now there were devout Jews from every nation
under heaven living in Jerusalem. And at this sound
the crowd gathered and was bewildered, because
each one heard them speaking in the native language of each. Amazed and astonished, they asked,
"Are not all these who are speaking Galileans? And
how is it that we hear, each of us, in our own native
language?" (vv. 1–8)

The end of one world and the beginning of a second.

On the Pentecost that came after Christ's passion, resurrection,
and ascension, God's Spirit descended with fire and wind in a way
both cohesive with all of his work from the beginning of creation, yet
also unique in his relationship with humanity. God was doing a new
thing, and it was first viewed, glittering and shaking above the earth,
from a little room in Jerusalem.

The long-promised Spirit came. And along with a whole new
fiery chapter of God's work to indwell and empower his people, a
simple but earth-changing thing happened, forever marking the
story of the universe. God upended Babel.

For the first time in the biblical narrative since the practically
prehistoric plain of Shinar, a gathered humanity spoke to one another
and were *understood*.

Babel upended but not *reversed*, you'll notice. It's better than
that. God does not just restore humanity to a single language.

Rather, as Mary and the Eleven, and all the rest of the first believers rushed downstairs into the cream-and-gold streets of Jerusalem on the morning of the great feast, bubbling, effervescent like new wine, the gathered peoples from the corners of the earth heard them each in his or her own language.

The healing miracle came to salve the old wound of Babel, but not quite as we expected. Not in the bringing of a superficial unity, but through miraculously binding together the many tribal threads that had long ago been ripped out of the one human cloth, without diminishing their individual colors and textures, without muddying their unique beauty. Those who heard the pure speech of the Spirit's people on that day had black eyes and brown and blue, with skin as many shades of brown and tan as there are kinds of sand on the beach. They were urbanites and cosmopolitans, farm kids and day laborers, the rich and the poor and the everybody.

IF ALL THE PLACES WHERE THE SPIRIT'S
HOLY FIRE BURNS WERE TO BE WRITTEN
DOWN, THE WORLD ITSELF COULD NOT
HOLD THE BOOKS THAT WOULD BE MADE.

When the Spirit spoke pure speech through the throats of Christ's people, he did not return to some original Adamic tongue. He simultaneously spoke to the multitude in *their* languages, the many languages of Babel, the tongues of their own hearts. The speech of their birth.

The unschooled Galileans, Luke tells us, spoke without stutter to those from faraway Parthia and Media, from Elam, from Mesopotamia. They spoke to Jews and Cappadocians, to those who had traveled to Jerusalem from as far as Pontus and Asia, to ethnic Phrygians, and Pamphyllians, Egyptians, Libyans, Romans even, Cretans, and Arabs.

Some heard them telling ceaselessly of the works of God. Others thought them daytime drunks, into a bottle of the good stuff at an ungodly hour of morning. But all present in the streets of Jerusalem heard the same truth that called out "Brother! Sister!" to all of humanity down the alleys.

What truth?

That any language, the world over, can burn with the pure speech of God.

Long after Babel but long before that Pentecost day in Jerusalem, even before Israel's exile, a man tasted the fire of purified speech.

In the year that King Uzziah died, when the prophet Isaiah stood in awe looking at the trailing glory of God filling the temple, he cried out "Woe!" in the presence of the six-winged seraphim, for he was truly undone. "I am a man of unclean lips," he said, "among a people of unclean lips," and his eyes beheld that which was not to be lightly looked upon (Isa. 6:5).

Isaiah's human proximity to glory revealed taught him that God's glory is a burning glory, and he knew that no divine message could rest in a mouth like his that was not yet purified. The burning, prismatic beauty of God sweeps all before it, either catching it up into its own holiness or consuming it utterly, like fire burns dead leaves.

But in the vision, Isaiah saw a seraphim (itself a "wind," or a "flame of fire," according to Hebrews 1:7) pluck a live coal from the altar, carry it down, and press it against Isaiah's lips with an announcement of cleansing and forgiveness.

Do you know what puzzles me about this story? Isaiah's fear and healing did not come to his eyes nor to his hands, feet, mind, or even his heart. The prophet was terrified in the presence of the Holy One because his *mouth* was dirty, backward, unclean.

And his cleansing came when his lips were touched by the fire of God.

Saint Macarius, in his fifth recorded homily, preached that on Pentecost, "fire ... worked in the apostles, when they spoke with fiery tongues." He continued brilliantly: "It was this fire which shone by the voice round St. Paul; enlightening his mind, but blinding his sense of sight; for not without the flesh did he see the power of that light. It was this fire which appeared to Moses in the bush. This fire, in the shape of a chariot, caught up Elias from the earth."[1]

He could have continued to speak of the pillar of fire that led the exodus through the wilderness; of flame on Sinai, Horeb, and Carmel; of flame after flame in the canon of Scripture and burning still in the church.

But what is the point in writing, trying to keep up with a fire whose borders spread across the earth faster than I can either perceive or type them? If all the places where the Spirit's holy fire burns were to be written down, the world itself could not hold the books that would be made.

The great and sad irony is that Pentecost, the single most unitive moment of human history, causes to this day such division. The Spirit's presence among his people, his ways and means of working, his revelations to the "me" and to the "us" are, from no fault of his, prone to spark the gunpowder we all carry around inside.

THE SPIRIT GIVES DIFFERENT GIFTS
TO DIFFERENT PEOPLE, AS HE ALONE
SEES FIT, AND ONLY AND ALWAYS FOR
THE PROPAGATION OF LOVE IN THE
CHURCH AS A SIGN TO THE WORLD.

A question of the Spirit helped prompt the Great Schism between Rome and Byzantium, dividing the Western church and the Eastern. Add to this the dozens of rifts and micro-rifts between mystics and rationalists, between sacramentalists and the more low-church, between charismatics and cessationists, and we begin to carry a burden.

Since the beginning of the charismatic and Pentecostal movements in the early twentieth century, many tears and much ink have been spilled over understanding of the gift commonly called "tongues." A sign gift, given to the church to point to the miraculous work of the Holy Spirit in the church, it has been interpreted and misinterpreted, used to refer to languages of prayer, to supernatural gifting in human languages, even to supernatural gifting in one's own language.

Some Christians say the gift of tongues has ceased, along with other miraculous giftings. Some Christians say it *should* persist, but they have never really heard it used well. Some say you bet it persists—would you like to hear it and have it for yourself?

PURE SPEECH IN THE SPIRIT IS LOVE, GIVEN WHATEVER VOICE IS BEST SUITED TO THE SITUATION.

Voices clamor and multiply, and whatever sign the gift of the Spirit might have brought us, it seems to have been lost somewhere in a scattering, in a confusion, in a second Babel. Is this really the gift of the Flame of Pure Speech, who blesses his people with clean lips for worship and glory?

The Spirit, I am convinced, gives different gifts to different people, as he alone sees fit, and only and always for the propagation of love in the church as a sign to the world. What he gives to some as a language for prayer or for messages of edification (if interpreted among the church), I am convinced is real, from the evidence of Scripture and from experience.

But in my own life, I have rarely experienced this, and (like Paul) feel that, though it is to be desired, as all the gifts of God are, there are things we should desire more greatly still—specifically, the clear speech of the Spirit among the people of God and as a sign to those seeking Jesus.

I have felt this in conversations specially visited by God, in teaching classes, in (once or twice) leading a gathering in prayer or worship. Whatever the setting, at the moments in my life when I have felt most in tune with the Spirit's will and voice, moments when I have felt that it was not I alone who spoke or wrote or dreamed or thought, but that I (as Peter said) was being "carried along" by the Spirit, the mode or method or language used as a means truly mattered very little to me. It didn't matter whether I spoke or heard in a language that I did or did not understand with my mind. The point of it all was that the Spirit wished to do something with words, in my life or another's, and he lit me or another on fire to be his voice. It is a feeling not quickly forgotten, and whatever realities the gift (or gifts) of tongues encompasses, it is that feeling, concrete yet abstract, that I suspect all who encounter it will share.

Moments like this have shown me the true power of Pentecost, of the Spirit's will and ability to draw us together. The moments when my mouth is moving but God's words are coming out.

Pure speech in the Spirit is *love*, given whatever voice is best suited to the situation, to the hearers. Whatever voice that is, like the Spirit who can even groan and have it mean something before the Father, is as predictable and as unpredictable as the wind in the apple tree.

Unity and division, speaking with and speaking against, are the very heartbeat of the Spirit's purification of our speech. Pentecost, seen this way, becomes more than just a happy arrival. It is part of a huge human story that stretches from a half-built tower on the plain of Shinar to you and me, the chosen of God yet scattered across the world.

Where our race has been united against God, in word or deed, let us always be scattered, pulled apart, confused. Where he wishes us to be gathered together to burn as one holy fire, let us blaze with the glorious patchwork union of diversity, born into one nature, baptized into one faith, made alive by the one Spirit of Christ Jesus, who pushed out of his grave, overpowered every enemy, and cooked fish for his friends by the waters.

The Spirit teaches us to speak as he did, to speak with love, pure and true as fire.

As we learn to speak as one, to burn as one, to dream as a people from all places speaking different tongues but the same speech, may we be warmed by the fire that Christ himself burned with, lit by the same light, anointed in each of our foreheads with the sealing of the same holy oil.

The life of the Spirit, the leading of the people of God into "pure speech," is the gift of Pentecost. And the implications of this for you and me are very close to limitless. What the Spirit did that day was to create a community that for the first time found the fibers of its unity woven warp and woof into a pattern of dynamic diversity.

The Jews, builders of walls and unrighteous keepers of the law, were the match that set all of humanity aflame in a moment. But that good fire did not crackle on each with the same sound. Just as there is one kind of burning for hickory, another for fir, others for apple, oak, rowan, and vine maple, the flame of pure speech sets each nation, tribe, and tongue and each one of our mouths alight in a different way.

To God there is a kind of burning of the spirit that happens when the heart of a Cherokee is set alight, another for the heart of a Magyar, another still for a New Zealander. Englishmen have a kind of burning, as do the Hmong and the Nez Perce. There is a burning for the Inuit and the Italians, the Argentines and Quechua, the Spanish and every tribe of the Amazon forests. We could list the clans of the whole earth here, each with their way. And one, the oldest (that of Jesus himself), for the Jews, from whose fathers and mothers salvation moved toward Bethlehem.

OH, THE UNITY OF DIVERSITY, THE
BEAUTY OF A GARDEN WITH ONE VINE
BUT MANY FLOWERS, THE STRENGTH
OF ONE BODY BUT MANY MEMBERS.

There is a kind of burning for you, for me, and for every individual human ever made. We each, because of our giftings, our personalities, our thousand unique kindnesses and potentials, have the capability to show and carry the Spirit of Jesus in a way recognizable with all the others but unique to ourselves. For that, he came.

There is one fire. One Spirit. But hallelujah, there are many burnings among the human family, and each one is welcome on the joyous altar of God.

Oh, the unity of diversity, the beauty of a garden with one vine but many flowers, the strength of one body but many members. The strangeness of a God who gives himself without limit. He gives his very essence away and is not diminished; he grants portions of his eternal power to creatures of blood and clay and is not weakened; he uses children, women, and men to be the pottery holding his infinite holy oil, and no matter how lavishly he pours himself into them, his vessel is always full. He speaks, and pure words only multiply from the echo.

Watching this mystery for eons, the six-winged seraphim cry to God over the altar, as they cover their feet and their faces:

Holy, holy, holy!
Holy, holy, holy!
Holy, holy, holy!

All this is the promise of pure speech by the Spirit. The promise of Pentecost.

"If you want to build a ship," Antoine de Saint-Exupéry said, "don't drum up the men to gather wood, divide the work, and give orders. Instead, teach them to yearn for the vast and endless sea."[2]

Many theological understandings of Pentecost see it as some pragmatic extension of wood gathering. The "power from on high" that Jesus promised is perceived primarily as a means to an end— the evangelization of the world. The thinking is that in the face of a humanly impossible mission (making disciples and baptizing unto the ends of the earth), a divine resource is needed to carry out orders.

LIPS THAT HAVE BEEN MADE PURE CANNOT BUT SPEAK OF THE WORK OF GOD.

Of course Pentecost is power-giving. But its means of power is not just the transfer of ability or capacity, but the lighting of desire. It was an act of God that taught us to yearn for the vast and end-less deep. More than the Spirit as some impersonal fuel for our "gas tanks" or a yes-man helper for missionary workers, God the Spirit, as intimate in the souls of Christ's people as breath in the lungs, teaches us to yearn, to desire, to burn alive with a holy passion.

It is this yearning that leads us to worship and disciple in "spirit and in truth." This is the yearning of the beloved church for her Lover, the call of the heart that makes such a life, such a love possible.

Lips that have been made pure cannot but speak of the work of God. Feet and hearts and minds touched by the fire of God cannot but go and make disciples and teach and baptize. Not simply because the power is there, but because the yearning burns there. Pentecost makes our yearning for heaven like the memory of a flavor, spiced and aromatic, that the tongue has tasted once—and knew in that moment it had brushed the one thing in all the universe it had been made for.

Pentecost is the kindling, the happy pileup, teaching us to want the very power of heaven to descend on each and all of us, on every possible permutation of humanity that runs in God's image over the face of the world. Pentecost is the fulfillment of a promise but also the making of a second promise, a fiery one of a good vagueness, one that must be perceived with the heart, tasted by the tongue, before it can be related by the mind.

PENTECOST IS A FLAME LIT ON THE SCATTERED EARTH, CALLING US … TO COME TOGETHER IN THE UNITY OF DIVERSITY.

Pentecost is fire that consumes and wind that whips the good flames higher. The church is a bush aflame, a bush that burns yet is not consumed, from which God speaks to the whole world without division or preference, in witness to his work of restoration, of redoing. Pentecost is glory come, the Spirit's high feast of firstfruit harvest. Pentecost is the Holy Spirit's exultant "It is begun!" ringing out in clean harmony with Christ's victorious "It is finished." It is a light set for the nations, a knocked-over lampstand that has splashed its oil to set ablaze the whole good earth.

We, the scattered peoples of Babel, are made one, baptized in flame, burnished into a reflection of the Father, the Son, and the Spirit of love who reigns among us.

Pentecost is a flame lit on the scattered earth, calling us to be cleansed in mouths, to come together in the unity of diversity. It is a fire on the dead ziggurat of Babel. It is a beginning of the new beginning, and a mighty good one, flaming out in every language heard by human ear.

It is the breath of life, formed by lips that have been cleansed by God.

Does that set your heart on fire?

THE OIL OF HOLINESS

Anointed with the Spirit Who Sanctifies

O God, who tells the number of the stars,
and calls them all by their names,
Heal, we beg of you, the contrite in heart,
and gather together the outcasts.

—Prayer from the Sarum Breviary, circa eleventh century

We Christians have no veil over our faces; we can be mirrors
that brightly reflect the glory of the Lord. And as the Spirit of the
Lord works within us, we become more and more like him.

—2 Corinthians 3:18 (TLB)

And now that you don't have to be perfect, you can be good.

—John Steinbeck, *East of Eden*

English ivy is the worst plant in the world.

It is invasive in my land and endowed by nature with nigh supernatural tenacity and growth. A sickly green menace, a demon disguised as flora, the ivy infests forests, strangling out native species above and beneath the soil, able to turn even the most rugged Douglas fir into a withering snag.

I have seen vines of the stuff as thick as my wrist, slithering hair-like day-roots to cling to the bark of its host, climbing to bunch and bundle itself like a fabled rat king in the treetop canopy. On the ground it spreads like spilled vomit, putrid and cloying, a home suitable only for pests and rot. It is good for neither fuel nor food nor any healthy thing, picturesque among the mosses on the wall of an old manse, perhaps—but down to its roots, a mad, devouring death of a plant nonetheless. It is packed with falcarinol, irritating some people's skin. Oregon has banned its import or sale in our state, but far too late to save many patches of pristine woods from going up in ivy.

How I hate it.

It's partly personal—the land that our home sits on has persistent swaths of the ivy. It snakes about in tendrils of all shades of health and flimsy decay, from stringent green to indeterminate grays that mottle the soil. You see the stuff throughout the east of our county, historic scenic forests slowly swallowed by the fecund wickedness of Satan's favorite weed-child.

English ivy (*Hedera helix*) has a lot going for it, from a "survival of the fittest" point of view. It grows quickly, on any surface or soil, needing few nutrients, able to survive in full sun or the barest light that filters down through the old growth. It has no natural predators that I am aware of, yet its mature blue-black berries are just edible enough to tempt birds to eat them, spreading new seeds in their droppings. It is not particularly vulnerable to insects, disease, or fungus to halt its increase, and its natural life span is far more than adequate to reproduce itself a hundredfold like something from a parable of hell.

Added to all this is the quality that makes it most like pure sin in botanical form—English ivy has acquired a strength beyond strength.

On their own the tangled vines are brittle and weak—deceptively weak, giving up to a gloved hand nearly without a fight. I can easily bundle five or six vines together in my hand, curse them blue (an important part of the process!), and rip them from the earth. But they are cunningly sectioned, designed to segment when subjected to stress.

Every bit that snaps and falls, down to the barest inch of vine, is capable of independent life. In a few days the pieces will sucker into the ground, sending down roots, sending up leaves, forming a new dynasty of evil. You must burn the vines, hang them on fences or branches to dry, or spread them out on gravel or pavement to keep from breeding your enemy through the very process that you intended to destroy it.

The sin and darkness of our lives have strength beyond strength. However entrenched they may feel, they are rotten at the core, often snapping when tugged, giving the false impression that with just a little more effort, a little more work, we might be able to win. But the truth is that their tenacity comes not from merely clinging to you, but from falling apart on you, breeding through brokenness, and suckering down into the heart while all the time you feel that you're fighting a winning battle.

Defeating them requires fire.

What do you think sin is like?

The metaphors that Christians choose for our iniquities tell us a great deal about our concepts of holiness, and more still about how we think the Spirit leads us into the life of Jesus.

Do we talk about sin as the breaking of a law? If so, then holiness means the keeping of laws after Christ's appeasement of the Judge of heaven. Is sin sickness? If so, then holiness means cultivating spiritual health after Christ's healing of every wound and illness through his power as the Great Physician. Is sin captivity? If so, then holiness means freedom after Christ's deliverance from all forces of evil that imprison us.

You see the pattern. If sin is life in the dark, then holiness is life in the light. If sin is straying like sheep, then holiness becomes following the Shepherd. If sin is dying in the lie, then holiness is living in the truth. If sin is being born into the lineage of the Devil, then holiness is adoption into the family of God. If sin is emptiness and void, then holiness is substance, the fullness of Christ. If sin is thorn and fruitlessness, then holiness is a harvest, lush and abundant.

All of these pictures for sin and holiness are found in Scripture, though we hear and think more about one or another of them depending on our Christian tradition.

Sin is all of these things, of course. More too.

WHAT WE THINK SIN IS WILL SHOW US WHAT WE THINK HOLINESS MUST BE.

Sin is a sickly sweet flower with leaves of skin and roots of clotted hair, pollinated by snakes, perfumed with corruption, bearing as many deathly petals to weep over as there are wickednesses in the world. Sin is *Hedera helix*, English ivy.

Holiness? Turning up the bed of the heart, uncovering every evil root, replanting.

What we think sin is will show us what we think holiness must be, and that in turn will tell us something of what the Spirit, the oil of holiness, will actually do to bring Christ's life to our life in the process we call sanctification.

God, I am convinced, is able to do whatever he chooses. But that belief only makes it more difficult to ask why a holy God does not instantaneously deliver a people called by his name, bought by his blood, and sealed by his Spirit. Instead, he holds us in tension, stretched like spider silk between the branch of the real and the window of the ideal, hanging between what is here and the world as it will be one day. Hanging there, with our virtues and vices in naked display.

Sin is an invasive species of the heart, breeding even as it is pulled up, designed for tenacity, for entrenchment, for getting its roots into you and acting as though it will be there until the seven bowls are poured out on the earth. Sin is segmented cruelly, sectioned to break if you try to pull it, made to make grief, to cause trouble, to apply to your life in every area that it touches the grief and pain and tragedy and sweat of the original curse. Pull up what you will, at some moments all seems well, while in others it seems to be a botanical Hydra, doubling its heads every time you decapitate it.

Why does God not simply deliver us with a wave of the divine hand? He could, you know. At least I believe he could. And yet like so many other processes that are slow and painful, he seems to think that great good can come from growth that is not immediately or obviously miraculous, from deliverance that is all done yet hardly at all worked out, from a path of holiness that is more like the ascent of a mountain by foot than by helicopter.

From the beginning of the church, Christians appropriated the practice of anointing in keeping with the ancient custom of the Jews. The very phrase מָשִׁיחַ (*mashiach*), Hebrew for "messiah," means "anointed one," and when brought forward into the Koine Greek trade language of the New Testament people of God, the title became Χριστός (*Christos*), a word used for commoner's olive oil, for the "chrism" of putting that oil on a special person as a mark of meaning and honor. "Christ" is thus not a proper name at all but a title: the Anointed. The one who has received the mark of oil.

One of the great mysteries is God's choice to extend the anointing of the Holy Spirit to every member of Christ's body. In no way diminishing the unique role of Jesus, we must affirm with the New Testament that his anointing is ours. As members of Christ's body, we join him in the unity of nature and purpose that he prayed for in John 14–16, our own heads dripping with the holy oil poured lavishly on him, the oil of holiness, like the rich oil that fires an ancient lamp and brings light to a darkened room.

You and I, and all of God's people from every age and nation of the earth, have been redeemed by the Messiah of Israel, the promised sprout of Jesse, the Word made flesh. He is our pattern, our stamp, as it were. We are made in his likeness just as our old selves were made in the likeness of Father Adam, and for all of those being remade and renewed as the creation groans around us, his nature is more truly our nature than any other thing about us.

Being made holy, being sanctified, is simply being made into the likeness of Jesus, the Holy and Anointed One. And it is the one whom Acts calls "the Spirit of Jesus" who naturally does that work, forming and stamping and pruning and burning and planting and causing us to prune and burn and plant ourselves.

Of this mysterious, unitive anointing, Paul spoke in 2 Corinthians 1:21–22: "It is God," he said, "who establishes us with you in Christ, and has anointed us, and who has also put his seal on us and given us his Spirit in our hearts as a guarantee" (ESV). For the anointed ones of God, who are all those in Jesus from every age, place, and station of humanity, the Spirit is not only a means of holiness and sanctification but a "seal," a "guarantee." Why is a guarantee needed? Because the process, as we've already seen, that God has chosen to redeem and sanctify the groaning world, to redeem and sanctify us, is exactly that: a *process*. The fact that it seems slow and messy, difficult and even discouraging in no way diminishes the fact that it is real, that it is happening.

Like the movement of glaciers, the shift of tectonic plates in the crust of the earth, the forces reshaping the world are happening all around us, rushing toward the final moment of happy catastrophe, but not static until then. They are changing things; they are changing us; we are changing things; we, in the Spirit, are changing us. For we, in Christ, through the Spirit of holiness, are God's anointed ones.

Knowing our weakness, the Father has given us a down payment for the full redemption that is coming. This down payment is the Spirit, whose presence and work we can ever look to in moments when we feel most keenly the gap between the now and the coming, the here and the not-here-yet, the thing that we have and the thing that we desperately need. He is here, the means of it, the guarantee of it. The lit lamp for the dark moments when all seems to be ivy and the fires are burning very low.

BEING MADE HOLY, BEING SANCTIFIED, IS SIMPLY BEING MADE INTO THE LIKENESS OF JESUS, THE HOLY AND ANOINTED ONE.

Christians have always used holy oil as a means of marking moments of particular importance in a believer's life—the anointing of the sick, as spoken of in the book of James, the anointing of the dying in the old practice of extreme unction, the anointing of new believers at baptism or confirmation. I myself, with my family, was anointed with oil on the forehead when my father was ordained as the pastor of a small Foursquare church. And I watched almost two decades later as my daughter and son were anointed immediately after their baptism. "You are marked by the Holy Spirit and sealed as Christ's own forever," our rector said as he crossed my children's heads with oil.

A statement of fact. A seal. A guarantee.

Every created thing brings forth fruit after its kind. From the matte-black pods of the purple sweet pea, which curl spring-loaded under the summer sun and burst at the brush of a boot, to the children of Adam, to the children of the second Adam.

"Fruit after his kind, whose seed is in itself," the King James Version reads in Genesis 1:11. "Fruit after his kind"—I can think of no better way to speak of the fruit of the Spirit. This is a doctrine as simple as any discussion of the birds and bees, and as intricate as every process of reproduction. That the ever-creating and sustaining Spirit should plant life wherever he is found is to be expected. But for all the consistency of his life-giving with his character, it is in every life as much a cause for awe and wonder as any birth. We may know the process as a basic litany of life for our species, but the everywhere-ness of birth does not subtract a hair of wonder from the mystery of two who become three.

The smell of a newborn child is an everlasting inheritance of humanity, passed to every generation before they are able to remember it for themselves, treasured only by those old enough to realize exactly what it is. It is the perfume of fruit-after-his-kind, the elemental smell of us, so soon lost, and yet being inhaled somewhere at every moment of history.

We must state the obvious now, but it is the obvious of the same kind as that of a child's birth, precious and mysterious. For the Spirit to bring forth life in you, "fruit," Paul calls it in Galatians, means that the Spirit who is himself a breath of pure life and a spiration of pure love will bear in you fruit in keeping with his nature. The fruit—love, joy, peace, long-suffering, gentleness, goodness, faith, meekness, temperance—is not simply a housewarming present brought by the indwelling God, it is fruit produced in you by the Father-gardener, in the earthiest and most precious manner, fruit-after-his-kind.

Thus, the portion of the Spirit's fruit that is love is love produced in you after the Spirit's kind. It is God's kind of love, with all the elemental giving and receiving that God knows and makes after his kind. The joy of the Spirit's fruit is God's joy; the long-suffering, the gentleness, the goodness are God's; the faith is God's; the potent meekness of the Spirit is God's; the steady self-control of temperance God's also.

"What is born of the flesh is flesh, and what is born of the Spirit is spirit," Jesus told Nicodemus in John 3:6. And yes, what the Spirit plants and waters is spirit, as surely as apples bear apples, and olives bear olives, and rose hips hold a thousand roses under the bloodred skin.

This is why God delights to call his redeemed brothers with Jesus the "firstborn." I used to balk a bit when the Bible used the term for God's Anointed One, implying that his anointing with holy oil extended to his people. Doesn't it seem a bit presumptuous? "King" I can understand, "adoptive father," "brooding mother hen," "conqueror." But older brother? Surely not.

But there can be no other way. The whole church, made by the Spirit into Christ's one body, built by the Spirit into a single temple resting on the Cornerstone, must be made of the selfsame anointed nature as that of Jesus. It is a profound mystery, without doubt, but it is an inevitable one for the God who seeks to see himself born infinitely in the eyes of the human family. Male and female, we were made in his image in the beginning, were purchased by his image whom we strung on the cursed tree, and are conformed into his image every day that the Spirit's fruit is born and borne in us. In limitless grace we are fruit after God's kind, Father, Son, and Holy Spirit. Some may be further germinated than others, but just as grains of wheat that fall into the earth and die hold all the promise of limitless harvest under the husk, so do we, or at least this is what the Spirit would have us believe. And to aid belief? Well, one of us has borne fruit already, a tree big enough to heal the nations, and his name is Jesus of Nazareth, and his nature is yours, Paul said, if you have been buried with him.

All sons and daughters of God who look to Jesus as Lord and Older Brother share in his nature through the sanctifying Spirit, the rich oil of holiness.

Now, though, we must live like it in a fallen world.

Say that you managed to clear an entrenched patch of English ivy from your land. The ground is bare and brown now, the ivy bed having murdered all other vegetation.

You may have won the battle, but if that's the limit of your vision, then your land won't be healthy. It will take more than the work of a sickle and bonfire to help the ground flourish. You need to plant or the ivy will return, and worse than before. Wait three days and all will still seem quiet, but in a week, maybe three, you'll see the first remnant returning, pruned into anger.

If you leave your ground bare, the ivy may have lost for a while, but you will not have won particularly much of anything.

Good must be cultivated. Life must be cultivated. Ripping up sin is a process that removes harm, and this is rightly called "sanctification," being made holy. But likewise, the *introduction* of postures, practices, attitudes, emotions, liturgies, habits, and everything that makes up life in the Spirit is also sanctification. Both of these, the tearing and the planting, are the Spirit's work to make you holy, anointed as the Anointed One of David is, with the cleansing holy oil of the Spirit.

Jesus was nearly killed after standing up in the synagogue of Nazareth and reading from the prophet Isaiah:

> The Spirit of the Lord is upon me,
>   because he has anointed me
>   to bring good news to the poor.
> He has sent me to proclaim release to the captives
>   and recovery of sight to the blind,
>   to let the oppressed go free,
> to proclaim the year of the Lord's favor.
>   (Luke 4:18–19)

"Today this scripture has been fulfilled in your hearing," Jesus, our Older Brother, said (v. 21), and his townspeople tried to bundle him up like ivy and hurl him off a cliff. In reality they were the ones in danger of a precipice—the sheer height of the truth, that God had anointed himself a man worthy of the oil of the Spirit, a man who was turning the whole earth up for replanting. Where the effects of sin were poverty, he was bringing the riches of holiness; where they were captivity, he was leading an exodus; where they were blindness, he was healing eyes; where they were oppression, freedom. Why? The Spirit on the Anointed One.

I am tempted to consider the process of holiness largely as a science of absences. What does living a holy life mean? Merely the removal of sin, I too often think, vigilance with sharp sickles of the soul and herbicides of the heart.

But holiness is really a science of *presences*. It is learning to know and cultivate the on-earth-as-it-is-in-heaven life of God in our lives. It is the presence of character and wisdom, of every kind of love. It is the very presence of God the Holy Spirit, leading one to Jesus, leading one to the Father.

It is the presence of true life.

Most of us recognize this truth, but the discord between this vision and our practical life jars us.

Why is it that we have such difficulty moving into spiritual maturity? If God the Holy Spirit is truly the ward of our lives, is he such a poor worker so as to let us wander and wallow in the same crass sins for decades rather than lead us into fruitfulness and a holy life?

Here I must stretch again to understand the goal of holiness. To extend the metaphor, it is not enough to have my earth cleared of the ivy of sin. It is likewise not enough to be planted in lush righteousness, fruitful with a bounty of the Spirit's own fruit. Holiness is not merely being planted, it is *planting*, plowing and planting myself, if such an awkward picture can be allowed. God does not merely want my righteousness. If he did, the briefest flash of a word from the Almighty and I would be perfected in an instant, into whatever completion our race may attain. He would rather wait, like the old farmer he is, to see me engaged in the work.

That is like him, good in the way he is good—a good that is not easy.

HOLINESS IS LEARNING TO KNOW AND CULTIVATE THE ON-EARTH-AS-IT-IS-IN-HEAVEN LIFE OF GOD.

If it is any comfort to us suffering sinners, God demanded this of himself. What was Christ doing in the desert if not pruning his temptations? Hebrews says (I paraphrase a little) that he took on every temptation that we tangle with, saw every shoot of evil that sought to root in his soil, "yet without sin" (4:15). If he was not willing merely to wave his hand and miraculously dismiss the sin that crouched at the door, why would we expect it in our lives? No, he *wrestled* it, through forty days of low blood sugar and forty nights of sleepless listening to desert beasts evaluate the nutritional content of his skin and bone out in the dark wastes.

The persistent need for both cutting and planting, for killing sin and planting righteousness according to its season, becomes a comfort. In the work of it, the tangling with thorns of it, I learn to know, to grow. I learn what it is not only to be a field but to be a farmer, not only to be planted but to be a planter. I learn to grow into the image of God, who in Christ Jesus, through the Spirit of life, whispers down wickedness slowly, patiently, and whispers up righteousness like a shoot of an olive tree, knowing that in the green weakness is the hope of fruit, and shade, and golden oil.

The Christ of the desert was holy from the beginning, but he also learned obedience through the things he suffered. Incarnate God? Yes, but as a human, Jesus forced himself to learn obedience, embracing the process, limiting himself through need, through boundary, through discomfort, through the long stretch from dark place to bright place that burns mind and muscle.

His way is hard.

His way is good.

The mystical Welsh puritan Morgan Llwyd wrote (in *Gweithiau*) something of what it feels like to hear the Spirit's voice call one into the life of Jesus. Here's an English translation:

> When the true shepherd speaks, and a man hears
> him, the heart burns within, and the flesh quakes,
> and the mind lights up like a candle, and the con-
> science ferments like wine in a vessel, and the will
> bends to the truth: and that thin, heavenly, mighty
> voice raises the dead to life, from the grave of

himself, to wear the crown, and wondrously renews
the whole life to live like a lamb of God.[1]

The Spirit of Christ the Shepherd, the son of David the shepherd, calls us into the life of a lamb, all the inner leaping that a farm kid like me recognizes.

I remember the December lambs, born in the Christmastide darkness of long winter nights. They came out wet, black or white, nearly able to stand. They smelled of copper. Cute as they were on wobbly hooves, they entered a world packed with fresh straw and danger. Many of them did not live to feel the spring sun.

Some we buried because a careless mother laid on or trampled them. Others we buried because a mad mother crushed them on purpose, according to some horrible logic of sheep that painted the ending of her line as some kind of evolutionary good (perhaps, given the circumstances, it was). Others went rigid and cold from lockjaw, the tetanus bacteria always flourishing in the dirt of the old barn, others from causes unknown. There was one, though, almost destined for death, that I helped save, and I will always remember her.

I was eight, I think. The new lamb was the runt of a set of triplets, a little black one, awkwardly strung between head and hooves. Her mother, feeling that her thin winter milk might feed two, but certainly not three, tried to kill her. Except for my parents' intervention, she would have succeeded.

We fed her formula from a great glass milk bottle with a sheep-sized red rubber nipple hanging off the mouth. For a while she slept in the mudroom of the farmhouse, needing, like a human infant, nearly constant milk, and the love of another warm-blooded creature to survive. We named her Baby.

The siblings for whom her mother nearly killed her both died of lockjaw within the week and were buried in the pasture. But the runt survived.

She thrived even, as the frosted months slowly melted away and the days lengthened toward equinox. By spring she went to graze with her cousins and murderous mother (who never again gave indication of either kinship or killing). Baby cropped the grass to ankle height under the gnarled trunks of the old pear orchard, her black back notable among the mostly white lambs, looking for all the world like any of the rest of the flock, except for one thing.

I'd stand at the fence and call her name, and her head would snap up from among the oblivious others, her lower jaw still rotating in the circular motion of cud chewers. Her orange eyes would search for us with oblong pupils, unblinking. Then, my face! Over to the fence she would trot, bounding faster with recognition, full of the simple interest of a herd animal who has heard the voice of one it loves.

Receiving that kind of love is a very good feeling. I think it is God's feeling.

I took Baby to Sunday school class for the teachers to use as a woolly object lesson about the Good Shepherd. In front of all the second graders, dressed in my best awkward black mock turtleneck (it was the nineties), I let Baby suckle my forefinger, as she loved to do, like an infant with a bony pacifier. As the teacher was talking about the sheep that know the shepherd's voice, Baby bit me for the first time, drawing blood, mingling it with her saliva.

Sometimes, receiving that kind of love is a very bad feeling. It can nip, draw blood even.

I think that also is God's feeling.

God does not want mere servants; he wants stewards. He does not call us slaves; he calls us sons and daughters. He does not only seek hands to do his bidding; he seeks anointed minds and hearts and spirits to actually stand up and do some of the bidding for themselves, as if it were his chief Anointed One himself who did it. He doesn't want prim little law keepers; he wants people who choose the way of love because they possess the nature of the Prime Lover.

The Spirit wants you to live, to truly live as God does (this is "being holy"), by your will, not merely by his. And like a good parent, ready at his child's elbow at any moment to help and guide, he allows mistakes to be made in service of that maturing good. He does not delight in the mistakes, but he delights in *you*, beloved one, and his grace is infinite, both in value and in depth. He allows time and process. He allows the brief aberration of a sin-scalded world that we are currently dealing with to become for us a classroom of maturity, sometimes teaching us lessons in tears, sometimes in blood.

But for all the participation that we are given in the living out of our own holiness, the work of sanctification is the Spirit's work, not our own. "No matter," John of the Cross wrote, "how much individuals do through their own efforts, they cannot actively purify themselves enough to be disposed in the least degree for the divine union of the perfection of love. God must take over and purge them in that fire that is dark for them."[2]

I HAVE A VISION OF WHAT CAN GROW HERE: APPLES, ROSES, LUSH THINGS, STRONG THINGS, USEFUL AND BEAUTIFUL AND GOOD THINGS.

The fire of purging, the "fire that is dark for them." The long night before morning, when births and murders and salvations happen. The night that reveals the brightness of stars and lampstands, bright precisely because the sun has not yet risen, bright precisely because the sun is already rising. This night removes; the morning will ask us to help the Spirit bring anew.

At those moments, the whole world shines in the brightness of God, a flame without smoke, a light that does not cast a shadow. Images flash in our mind, of sickles and poison, of bare earth, of the mystery of sprouts, of an ageless tree, of olives pressed under stone wheels turning like sundials, pressing our days out lavishly, caught in a clay jar, destined for someone's forehead.

I think that is what holiness is like.

Saint Augustine was a man who knew both unusual sin and unusual sanctification. One of his prayers to the Holy Spirit goes:

> *Breathe in me, O Holy Spirit,*
> *   that my thoughts may all be holy.*
> *Act in me, O Holy Spirit,*
> *   that my work, too, may be holy.*
> *Draw my heart, O Holy Spirit,*
> *   that I love but what is holy.*
> *Strengthen me, O Holy Spirit,*
> *   to defend all that is holy.*
> *Guard me, then, O Holy Spirit,*
> *   that I always may be holy.*[3]

I pray this myself as I wade through the ivy with a short sickle in my hand, slicing and snapping the vines, inhaling the metallic aroma of their cracking roots. They slap and twang; I pluck them like loose guitar strings. I gather all I can up from the ground in armfuls, barrowfuls. But the way of this process is that it is a *process*. I do my best at the work, piling the uprooted in great heaps away from fresh soil, awaiting a day of fire. But I know that in a few weeks, I will return here to find shoots sprouting where their parents grew strong. The hope is that at every return the invaders will be fewer and weaker than before.

Because every once in a while I have a vision of what can grow here: apples, roses, lush things, strong things, useful and beautiful and good things, reproducing lavishly after their kind. Abundance. The very good.

In my ground.

In my land.

In my world.

In my heart.

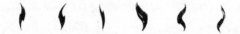

THE BREATH OF ONE BODY
Joining the Spirit Who Unifies

Has it ever occurred to you that one hundred pianos all tuned to the same fork are automatically tuned to each other?

—A. W. Tozer, *The Pursuit of God*

I ... beg you to lead a life worthy of the calling to which you have been called, with all humility and gentleness, with patience, bearing with one another in love, making every effort to maintain the unity of the Spirit in the bond of peace. There is one body and one Spirit, just as you were called to the one hope of your calling, one Lord, one faith, one baptism, one God and Father of all, who is above all and through all and in all.

—Ephesians 4:1–6

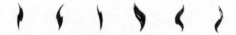

On the wall of my favorite East Portland sandwich joint hangs a signed black-and-white photo of Sid Vicious, bassist for the infamous Sex Pistols. The Prince of Punk, in one of his iconic shots (taken, legend whispers, by the Clash's Bob Gruen), stands shirtless, half-turned from the camera, eyes squinted. Blood from his face and breast runs down in clots and trickles, smudged in sticky fingerprints across his white Fender bass.

"Gimme a fix" is carved into Sid's chest (he did the carving himself before an unruly Dallas show). Sid stands there captured forever on film, swollen, bloody, angry, rebellious, punk as everything, ready for anything, full of all things rebel and awesome. Earlier generations had John Wayne and the cowboys to grow up with, individual and tall and violent and alone. Mine had the rockers, toting all the attitude that rode with a six-gun, but with a little more beat, a little more black leather instead of brown.

We all have our pet legends, our heroes or antiheroes, who stand for good or for evil, but who stand alone. I can't speak for anyone else, but in pioneer-strong Oregon, the people we revere, wish to emulate, are those who (like salmon) swim against the flow of the stream, who fight until it kills them (it killed Sid) to do things their own way. It is in my Western people's nature to love rebels.

It is for this reason that Sid Vicious—who in life was Sid the emotionally stunted, Sid the brutal, Sid the murder suspect, Sid the addict and the overdosed—is whom we long for an autograph from, whose photo we enshrine like that of a dead hero. There is surely a kind of beauty from lives like his, but it is the beauty of sad waste, like a Picasso set on fire for a few minutes' entertainment.

Gone in a red moment is something irreplaceable, infinitely precious.

But the photo still hangs there, timeless. "Gimme a fix."

With an imagination shaped by my culture to want to be Sid, the rebel, the flipper of fingers, how can I hope for unity?

When John the Baptizer spoke of the Lamb washed in the river, he said that while he (John) baptized with water for repentance, the one who was to come (the Lamb) would baptize with the Holy Spirit and fire. The old Greek word βαπτι'ζω (*baptizó*) used here is a simple one, meaning to immerse, to submerge. John's own hands baptized the Great Baptizer, and I suspect that he trembled as he pushed the head of his cousin from Nazareth under the Jordan.

"One baptism," Paul said in his mighty list of spiritual unifiers in Ephesians. Indeed, one baptism, and one Spirit. But to what baptism does this refer?

Acts 1:5 and 11:15–16 make it quite clear that whatever being baptized in Spirit and fire means, Pentecost is (at least the primary) fulfillment of it. "The beginning," Peter called the day of Pentecost, when he told the other first Christians of the way the Spirit was remaking their community, unifying Gentile and Jew.

In the most elemental sense, unity means affirming that you share another's story. Disunity, of course, is the reverse—denying that your story and the story of another are tied together. Denying that your interests might be the same, that what benefits and enlivens one might do the same for the other, that what harms the one cannot exist without hurting both.

As evidence of this principle, consider the great separations of the church. The Great Schism between the Eastern and Western church in 1054 resulted in the pope of Rome and the patriarch of Constantinople calling each other "anathema" (the ultimate denial of another's Christianity), a curse that was not reversed until 1965— and even then leading to no meaningful reunion. To this day, with only minor exceptions, these churches refuse to believe they share the same story. Similar is the Protestant Reformation, beginning as a movement for correction and purification of the excesses and absurdities of the Roman Church. For all the good it brought, the division led to murder, inquisition, massacre, and war after outright war, the deepest denials that the interests of the one side were woven in any way with the health of the other. Witness, too, the thousand and one severances of Communion leading to the situation we modern Christians, particularly Protestants, find ourselves in.

Ours is a world that can barely imagine all Christians, all partakers of the one baptism, sharing a single story. This, in spite of the theological affirmation that we are bound together by the Spirit into a shared bloodline, closer than any ties of family, nation, or neighborhood. We are utterly one. But do we live like it?

No. Instead of visible unity, we live in a patchwork Christian world of Methodists and Presbyterians, First, Second, and Third Baptists, Brethren, Mennonites, Amish, Copts, Foursquare, Assemblies of God, vanilla-flavored nondenominationals, Latin masses and English masses, services contemporary and traditional, emerging, emergent, emerged, but hardly ever *merging*.

Where did we lose our single story in the Spirit?

Can we ever get it back?

It is one of our great modern Christian losses that so many of us have so utterly forgotten the biblical imagination for the kind of world we live in. In keeping with our Enlightenment heritage, Protestants in particular, and evangelical Protestants even more so, have slowly slumbered into, if not a bad theological view, a dull, misleading one. We have somehow come to dream, to practically believe, even if our best theology still holds a more biblical memory, that what is most real is what can be most immediately seen.

But the Bible's theological imagination sees the whole world as a place of overlaps, of shared and blurred boundaries between what is commonly called "earth" and what is commonly called "heaven." Our universe is a place of extension and coextension, of all things being both fully what they appear (in contrast to false philosophies that paint the world as a place of duality, unreality, or illusion) and being infinitely more than they first appeared. In the biblical nature of things, we can say with Jacob (who laid to sleep on a stone in the desert and saw the house of God), "Truly the LORD is in this place. And I did not know it!"

Historic Christianity has called this concept the "sacramental" nature of reality, an understanding that God has made so-called spiritual things to overlap mightily with "physical" ones, so much so that those categories nearly (not quite) lose their meaning. This must be received before it can be understood. It must be tasted and known to be good, before any dream of analysis. This form of being that God has chosen is seen in the nature of Christ himself (the pattern of all re-creation), who is at once fully human and fully divine. It is seen in the nature of Christ's body and blood shared with all, experienced and remembered in the sign of Communion. It is seen in the waters of baptism, which receive us and give us back to the light, their mysterious power to transform coming not from our understanding but from the Spirit who presides over them, from our faith in his work, from the goodwill of the God of every element, of all signs.

Orthodox priest Father Stephen Freeman calls this way of seeing as God sees, this sacramental nature of reality, "mystical realism." I like the term. The mystically real seems a contradiction until we feel it, until we understand that God has made us to understand, has made us in our very natures as beings that must grasp—instinctively, eternally—to pull together flesh and spiritual life, the world of what is seen and the world of what the seen things mean.

Writing online in 2014, Freeman wrote:

> In the literalism of the modern world (where a thing is a thing is a thing), nothing is ever more than what is seen. Thus every spiritual reality, every mystery, must be referred elsewhere—generally to the mind of God and the believer. Christianity becomes an ideology and a fantasy.... The reality of in [sic] the Incarnate God was not obvious to those around Him: no surgery would have revealed His Godhood. The proclamation of the Gospel, from its most primitive beginnings ("the Kingdom of God is at hand"), announces the in-breaking of a mystical reality.[2]

Indeed, no surgery would have revealed the Godhood of Jesus. When in the throes of his passion the flesh of Christ's ribs was shredded by Roman flagellums, no glittering divinity underneath was exposed. When his side was pierced by the spear from below the cross, no inner *shekinah* blazed out, carrying the bitter world to ruin. His blood that soaked the dirt of Judea clotted and blackened and smelled of rot, as all human blood does, carrying no sign that it had begun the renewal of all things.

WE HAVE BEEN ADOPTED ALL TOGETHER INTO THE DIVINE FAMILY, BORN AGAIN AND FROM ABOVE INTO THE NEW NATURE OF CHRIST, BURIED AND RAISED NOT ONLY TO NEW LIFE BUT TO HIS KIND OF LIFE.

And yet the reality that was unseen was not unreal. Jesus of Nazareth is, in every sense and understanding of Christian theology, *God*. He is a sign to us, a living sign by the Spirit who is both symbol and the one pointed to. And in the same manner the gifts of his Spirit are signs, every one of them, pointing to realities that are mysterious but no less able to be joyously embraced, to be celebrated as the true life of the seen world.

If we do not understand that we live in a sacramental reality, we can never truly know ourselves. We are creatures made for the thing called "sacrament," made to perceive that beyond (not against) all rational dissection and inquiry, the waters from the creek in Oregon, from the well in Bangladesh, from the tap in Toronto, from the river in Budapest, can become the waters of the Jordan, ready to baptize Christ's body anew if we only ask, pouring them out in faith. We are made to sense that, whatever our thoughts about "real presence" in Communion, Jesus is *really with us* at the table when we partake of the bread and the wine.

It is inescapably Christian to look through the things that are seen to perceive those that are not, Christian in a way most primal. These are the contours of life in the Spirit, whether we recognize them or not. These are the bones of our shared story, the way our world has been made. The way that it is being remade. This is the foundation of the unity of the Spirit.

AS CHRIST TOOK ON HIMSELF OUR POVERTY, THROUGH HIS SPIRIT HE PLACES ON US HIS RICHNESS.

We have been adopted all together into the divine family, born again and from above into the new nature of Christ, buried and raised not only to new life but *to his kind of life*, which is sacramental, a sign and bridge between all real things, seen and unseen. Because of this, Paul was able to speak of the united body of Christ, single and whole, which was baptized in the Spirit and fire on Pentecost, and which extends to encompass every person who has, is, or will be "in Jesus" for the duration of eternity. "There is one body and one Spirit, just as you were called to the one hope of your calling, one Lord, one faith, one baptism, one God and Father of all, who is above all and through all and in all" (Eph. 4:4–6). This body becomes a mystical reality nearly as deep as the individual body of Jesus. Why? Because by sharing in the same Spirit, by being indwelt and filled by God's own personal and divine Breath of Life, we both become full partakers in Christ's resurrection nature, and yet …

And yet no surgery would reveal it.

This is our deepest single story—being joined bone to bone and spirit to Spirit to the very nature of God in Jesus, and that same nature in all his people. As Christ took on himself our poverty, through his Spirit he places on us his richness. In the way that he took up our death (and trampled it), he gives us the limitless life of his resurrection. He shared in our nature? In the Spirit we share fully in his.

This is the mystery of the church. If we, through faith in Jesus, have joined him in the death of baptism, his Spirit dwells in us, and his deathless life is our abiding destiny, because the Great Vine has borne fruit after his kind. If we, through faith in Jesus, have joined him in the death of baptism, we are seamlessly united with all who have called on, do call on, or will call on the name of the one who is the same yesterday, today, and forever.

One baptism. One body. One God and Father of all. One vine. Many, many clusters of fruit ripening for the Great Harvest Party.

One story.

Who are the Christians in my community whom I have wounded? Who has wounded me? How have I forgotten that the one Spirit of God unites me more closely with Christ's whole body than my bones are knit to my marrow?

Gimme a fix.

Oh, Spirit, show me your path to unity, and help me to walk it.

Whatever scars and wounds the one body of Christ might bear, in God's eyes there have been no amputations, no excisements of one part or another. To Jesus, all his family shares the same story, because his story is about the deepest part of that which no one can change—our family, our genealogy, our species, if you will, as fruit-after-his-kind.

ONE BAPTISM. ONE BODY. ONE GOD AND FATHER OF ALL. ONE VINE. MANY, MANY CLUSTERS OF FRUIT RIPENING FOR THE GREAT HARVEST PARTY.

This is rich, and strong. A very good teaching. A teaching of the very good. But while we may affirm it over and again, the reality is that we fail, daily, over the course of centuries, to live it among our churches, in our homes, between the many members of the One. The reality is that *I* fail by what I do and what I leave undone. I, the admirer of Sid in the sandwich shop, would often rather break fellowship than acknowledge hurt. I hold back from forgiving, hold back my confession and repentance when I have wronged others. I think of myself more highly than I should, and that skews every relationship inside the church and outside it. I point fingers accusing others, while I myself am guilty of the sins with which I charge them. I am divisive, hard to live with, judgmental.

I fail, I fail.

I can write paragraphs like this: "True unity, true ecumenism (the working for practical Christian unity in keeping with our theological reality) is a sign of profound spiritual strength. I can think of few things more difficult than to fight and bleed and draw blood, but still return to dialogue, to wash the wounds of the one you have wounded, to allow the 'enemy' who struck you to staunch your bleeding. It is strength and maturity to push beyond bristling at how brothers or sisters do or say something but still embrace them, feed them, be fed by them." But can I live such words? If I am honest with you, hardly ever.

Schism, for all its pain of parting, is easier than unity. While there is a time to part ways with those who deny the core tenets of Christianity as expressed in the old creeds, those times are very few, a last resort full of inexpressible pain and inevitable loss.

We need friction, sharp commitment to the teaching of Christ, life kept in keeping with the holy calling we've heard. But how lightly we sever ourselves from the great, shared single story. How quickly do we find some excuse to dismiss another's faith, another's inheritance in Christ, another's fruitful life in the one Spirit. How quickly conservative ostracizes progressive, progressive mocks liberal, Catholic bars Protestant from the Eucharistic table, how quickly East and West shout "Anathema!" at each other. How quickly do parish churches become two-parish churches, then four, eight, sixteen, in a process not of multiplication, but division, in which the sum of all parts is less than the whole. This is not the division of cellular growth, but of a cancer, each permutation becoming a mutation, each more prone to divide than its parent.

One story becomes a thousand.

I have helped make it a thousand. Sometimes I do not know where to turn, how to be healed, though my mind knows the answer.

Forgive me, Holy Spirit.

Is Christ divided?

In the Anointed One's great parting speech and prayer in John 14–17, he teaches his friends about the nature of abiding in his nature (that of the True Vine), and promises them that the Counselor, the Spirit of truth, will guide them into all truth, witnessing to the church and the world of all that the Father and Son have. In his prayer Jesus pleads at length before the Father on behalf of all those who will come to believe in him. There is no member of his body, from any age or any place, whom his intercession does not include. His words are the consecration prayer of the Great Priest over his clan, his kingdom of priests to come, every man, woman, and child who would cling to his name and receive his nature.

Jesus prayed, as recorded in John 17:19–23:

> For their sakes I sanctify myself, so that they also may be sanctified in truth.
>
> I ask not only on behalf of these, but also on behalf of those who will believe in me through their word, that they may all be one. As you, Father, are in me and I am in you, may they also be in us, so that the world may believe that you have sent me. The glory that you have given me I have given them, so that they may be one, as we are one, I in them and you in me, that they may become completely

one, so that the world may know that you have sent
me and have loved them even as you have loved me.

After the prayer Jesus crossed the Kidron Valley, and entered a
garden that may well have reminded God of Eden, to be betrayed
near an olive tree by his friend.

Even with the mob at his back in Gethsemane, the betrayer
Judas had a kiss for his Teacher.

My grandmother, a legendary local collector of antiques and curiosi-
ties, gave an 1850s print by John Everett Millais to my wife and me
for our wedding. It's large in its black frame, perhaps thirty inches or
more, and has hung in every home we've lived in.

The picture shows a young couple dressed in the French fashion
of the mid-1500s. They are in a walled garden, ivy clinging to the
stones behind them, clasped in one another's arms. The girl looks up
into the young man's face with pleading eyes, her hands tying a strip
of white cloth around the bicep of his left arm. The man gazes back,
his face both rejecting and reassuring, and with his right forefinger
he pulls apart the knot of cloth she seeks to tie.

An inscription, covered by the matte of our frame, reads:

A Huguenot
on St. Bartholomew's Day,
Refusing to Shield Himself from Danger
by Wearing the Roman Catholic Badge

A little cloying perhaps, but it's a scene imagined from real history. On St. Bartholomew's Eve in 1572 (during the height of the Wars of Religion), French Catholics, part of a twisting political intrigue masquerading as Christian piety, betrayed and massacred thousands of their Protestant neighbors—men, women, and children—flinging their bodies into the dark waters of the Seine.

The story of the picture is an imagined snapshot of the moments preceding the bloodbath. The girl in the print, a Catholic, has caught wind of the plot against her beloved's people. Desperate to save his life, she brings him the white cloth (the ID that ensured that the Catholics wouldn't slay each other), a cloth that can save his life, allow him to escape the coming three days of blood. He, knowing the danger, refuses—choosing the possibility of death rather than to be something other than what he is. In the picture the white cloth is stretched between his hands and hers, leaving the viewer to guess whether it remains tied to the Huguenot or whether it is left in the garden of ivy.

Christian killed Spirit-baptized Christian on the night of St. Bartholomew's Eve, betrayed and spilled blood ransomed by God onto the crying stones of Paris. Christian ears were deaf to pleas for mercy; heads that had been anointed by the Spirit of life were sliced callously from the necks that held them. Children baptized in the name of the Trinity were murdered before their parents, and parents before their children. All this in the name of the church, in the name of Christ, all for the cause of "righteousness."

All because Christians did not know how to live the one Spirit's story together.

Lest we think that such heartbreaking bloodshed between the people of the one baptism was left behind us before the Enlightenment, remember the Rwandan genocide of the 1990s. Have you heard the stories of Hutu priests and pastors betraying the helpless, opening the churches where Tutsis had fled for sanctuary to the mobs of their killers? Christians took to Christians with machetes and pitchforks, Christians burned Christians in their churches, Christians maimed and murdered and bulldozed and gutted Christians like so many sheep led to the slaughter, while all around the world, those members of the one baptism in more peaceful places read the words of Christ that rang for bloody weeks in cosmic irony: "I in them, and thou in me, that they may become perfectly one."

ONLY IF THE SPIRIT IS CALLED ON AND PARTNERED WITH CAN THERE BE ANY KIND OF PEACEMAKING, ANY KIND OF "FATHER, FORGIVE US, FOR WE KNOW NOT WHAT WE DO."

To list the crimes of Christians against Christians—the wars, the slaveries, the rapes, the abuses, the economic exploitation, the insults, the slander—would be impossible. To list every wound and division, intentional and accidental, is beyond human capacity to grasp, let alone to catalog, let alone to confess, repent from, grant absolution for. Only the Spirit who makes us one in the first place can draw us into unity, and only he knows the day or the hour when we will be restored, placed into the full reality that Jesus prayed for on the night of that first of so many betrayals.

Think of what it would take to bring reconciliation to such Gethsemanes. Only by the one Spirit could there ever be hope for such an absurdity. But in spite of the enormity of it all, we must still work in that same Spirit to unite the many peoples of the one baptism of Pentecost, in the hope of the power of Christ's prayer, in the hope of the power of the one Spirit, himself a breath of love, that gives life and meaning and voice to the whole body.

It is here that the Spirit's work takes on the character of a true miracle. While I feel that I, the admirer of Sid Vicious, have trouble with unity, this is an utterly human struggle. We all share it in our own way.

Only if the Spirit is invited to remake us, to re-create us, to help us remember and live out the beloved reality that our nature as people of the one baptism is to be one as the Anointed One was with God, only *then* will there be hope for any kind of reconciliation. Only if the Spirit is called on and partnered with can there be any kind of peacemaking, any kind of "Father, forgive us, for we know not what we do."

Only by the Holy Spirit, the one who unifies us.

And only *if.*

In spite of the monumental difficulties, the seeming impossibilities of union, to strive for anything less than the vision of Christ's prayer for his people in John 17 is to fall short of the vision and intention of God himself for humanity.

It is the honor and duty of every one of Christ's disciples to extend their hands not only to the world but to their brothers and sisters, across every division, wound, and boundary that history or life has driven between us. To do this, Protestants must look to Catholics for wisdom and guidance, and Catholics to Protestants. "Orthodox" believers of all varieties must humble themselves in keeping with the Spirit whom they remember so well in their liturgy, understanding that Christ's whole church is the community of the baptized and inheritors with them of the apostles' teaching and authority—no matter how distended the church may appear to be. All those who bar Communion to other baptized Christians must repent, confessing that they have sinned in keeping Christ's people from Christ's table and by holding as righteousness human divisions that have no place in the community of the Spirit. We must all cut off our arrogance, our bitterness, our pride, our memory of wrongs, our list of trespasses, our insults, our mockery, our profaning of things that another in the family of Jesus calls holy. We must work to think the best of all others, whether next to us in the pew or across the political aisle, recognizing that all who confess Jesus as the risen Lord and share in his nature are us, as surely as we are them, and as surely as we through the Spirit are in Christ, and Christ in God. Further, we must reach out in reconciliation, truth, repentance, and magnanimity to those who have wounded us and to those whom we have wounded.

We must die a hundred times to ourselves, making room for a new life of unity. We must bear fruit in keeping with our kind.

This mystery is the work of the one Spirit.

There's no more potent image for sharing your story with another than that of marriage. It's a *nature* thing. This is why God, in telling us what his love for humanity is like, uses the covenant language of marriage and sexuality to express his cleaving to his people, his union with humanity, his mingling of the divine and the human into the story of God. Like marriage, which John Chrysostom called "one flesh of purest gold," God protects and nourishes and refines his union with his people, our great shared story, with the conventions of promise. More deeply than any other relationship (except perhaps monastic life), the married life is a *covenanted* life, a *vowed* life. Through the weaving of promises meant to stand as strong as death itself, the bride and bridegroom pledge themselves utterly to one another, and in so doing, begin to tell a shared story so closely aligned that, like their very flesh, it is best thought of no longer as two but as one. The degree to which that story is lived faithfully, with health and integrity, is the degree to which any marriage union stands or falls.

This is the true tragedy of our modern culture of divorce, is it not? When we put asunder what God has joined together—whatever reasons legitimate or illegitimate there may be—it is not just the rending of hearts that can be heard and seen and felt; it is the rending of a story, of all the myriad possibilities to which life could have led the couple. Children who might have been born remain unconceived, future work and laughter and joy and shared sorrow all wither in a moment, a future that might have been beautiful dies as the unity dies, as the story dies. Whatever beauty and hope the couple have individually, whatever hope of reconciliation and renewal, they will always have might-have-beens.

This, the sense of the might-have-beens, is in the church too. It is not given to us to know what might have been if the Eastern and Western churches had chosen to embrace and seek the unity of the one Spirit instead of declaring one another cursed. It is not given to us to know what would have happened had Rome wept and repented at the protests of the priest Martin Luther, seeking to embrace reformation, to repair the wrongs, abuses, and errors that had snaked among the shepherds of Christ's flock. It is not given to us to know how any or all of us might be different in a world where the people of the one Spirit lived a little more like the people of the one Spirit should.

Neither is it given to us to know the other might-have-beens, either—what divisions have been averted by the Spirit that would have fractured us infinitely further. What is given is this: we are called to be one, as God himself, from all eternity, has been one, Father, Son, and Spirit. We are called to be fruit after our Father's kind, to be covenant makers, keepers of our true unity, protectors of our story.

Whatever our age, wealth, or skin tone, whatever our gender, language, or place of birth, we can be an utterly individual expression of the union of God with humanity. We can join with the whole, examples of diversity in the unity of the One, keepers of the story, protectors of Christ's prayer of promise that is so inexorable and so fragile. This is what it means to be a member of Christ's body through the Spirit.

Being a member of Christ's body is more than a pragmatic or functional reality, more than something good only for telling us what our "church" jobs might be. It is a sacramental reality first, a *nature* reality—the reality that you are even now being formed in the likeness of Jesus, in a mystical reality that at times is more visible than others but has become more real about you than any other thing that might make you *you*.

One baptism, one body.

One Spirit.

One story.

COME

Rising with the Spirit Who Calls

And all shall be well and
All manner of thing shall be well
When the tongues of flames are in-folded
Into the crowned knot of fire
And the fire and the rose are one.
—T. S. Eliot, "Little Gidding"

I turned to see whose voice it was that spoke to me, and on turning
I saw seven golden lampstands, and in the midst of the lampstands I
saw one like the Son of Man.... His voice was like the sound of many
waters. In his right hand he held seven stars, and from his mouth
came a sharp, two-edged sword, and his face was like the sun.
—Revelation 1:12–16

Once I briefly got lost in Croatia.

Two friends and I were staying in Zagreb, the capital city. It is a city that flows down from hills, the rising streets on the hillsides punctuated by the contrasts of so much of Eastern Europe—red-checkered cathedrals abutting utilitarian Soviet-era concrete apartment buildings. In the country beyond the city's outskirts, we'd passed field after minefield, rich farmland, grazing cattle, buildings pocked by old bullet holes. In the city, residents stared—this boyish American was wearing sandals on his feet in March!

A missionary in the city had taken us to a quiet street where a church-owned hostel room, an apartment within an apartment, was tucked up on a hill. There were no signs to mark it. "Come on in," our host invited. After ensuring we were well provided for, he said good-bye and drove away. We lay our backpacks on the bunks in the little room and splashed water on our faces. Energized, even though we were jet-lagged, we decided on a walk in the city and left the little place. Out we went, exploring, photographing, laughing, up and down the stony streets.

When dusk began to creep over the roofs, we realized we had no idea where we were. The twilight grew as we tried to retrace our steps, working, worming our way backward up a hill we thought we'd descended, passing a park with a familiar-looking fence (wait, didn't I take a picture of that lamppost?), and wandering down residential streets that were all so different they began to look the same. The darkness grew. Though we had no fears for our safety, as the stars came out we began to wonder if we'd be sleeping in the park that night. Our info, foolishly, was all back in our room. We had no cell phones nor the number or address of our friend who lived in the city.

We walked. All the roads we passed looked like the arms of a maze, a labyrinth with false ends and a closed roof, its lights flicking out one by one as the city shuttered up for the night.

We had been invited to this place, then welcomed by a friend, had been shown a kindly place prepared for us … and had promptly wandered off into the lostness like any unmet traveler. What good is even the kindest invitation if you cannot find the right door?

Our laughter had gradually turned to silence. We walked and looked with the tired quiet of travelers who fear their bunks may not be slept in on a dark winter night.

We turned, just as I thought about looking for an out-of-the-way bench or tree. We descended the street a little bit. The altered perspective was enough—we saw a familiar stairwell. Up we went, pulling the key from where it had been hidden. The door opened into the quiet room. We went in and rested, grateful that we'd not squandered our invitation as travelers in a strange city.

The invitation. This is the end. The perfect end.

And how often I take it for granted.

In this end there is very little to talk about. Words are not needed to inform or elaborate; they are not needed to argue or convince. All of that has been done, or tried at least. In the end, at the end, words do two things for those with ears to hear them: words *soothe* and words *invite.*

They soothe, like a kind and haunting lullaby at the close of evening. They remind us that we are not alone, that however dark the night may be, there is one near us who can see in the night, who does not slumber or sleep, the singer of songs who will chant up the sun. "Rest," his song goes. "Rest. Enter into your rest."

Words, here at the end, soothe, spoken by the Spirit who in nature and function is a guarantee of the full redemption that is to come. He is our seal, our down payment. He is the one who sings us into this rest, day unto day, night into night, deep calling unto deep at the sound of his waterfalls.

"Rest. Rest. Enter into my rest."

LONG AFTER WE HAVE RUN OUT OF
POSITIONS OR OPINIONS, THE WORDS
THAT HAVE ALWAYS STOOD MAY
BE HEARD MORE CLEARLY: "COME,"
THEY SAY. "COME AND SEE."

When the whole world seems full of monsters, writhing with unclean things, with beasts and dragons and fears from the sea and below the sea; when the blood of good people cries out from the ground; when there are no answers; when the sky is clouded, showing no sign of growing light, it is then that the weak strength of the Spirit's soothing song is most needed. He is, Paul said, our down payment of the resurrection life that is to come, to us and the whole world, the life that has come, though it may still be but seed-life, growing like an invisible plant in the trampled and borderland places.

Words soothe at the ever-present end. The Spirit soothes at the end.

Words invite too. Our universe is founded on the nature of a being infinite and relational; and the dynamic principles of governance that keep all in balance, the deepest physics behind all things, seen and unseeable, are those of asking—of invitation. This is the nature of God, three persons, from all of time engaged in a perfect and glorious process of inviting the other in himself, of loving the other in himself, of giving himself eternally, of receiving the eternal gift of love.

Here at the end, long after silence has fallen in the halls of argument and academia, long after we have run out of positions or opinions, the words that have always stood may be heard more clearly: "Come," they say. "Come and see. Come and know. Come and love and love and be beloved."

This is the eternal invitation of the Trinity to the Trinity, God in perfect union and diversity. This is the invitation extended from the Trinity, through the Spirit, to all who are partakers in the divine nature, all who begin to ripen as fruit after God's kind. This is the invitation that the Spirit brings to all who are being made into the likeness of Jesus.

The invitation to me, under the waters, neither sinking nor rising.

The invitation to you.

"Come."

John, the beloved disciple of Jesus who laid his head against the Teacher's chest on the night of the Last Supper, lived to be an old man.

Tradition says that he was the only one of Christ's faithful disciples who did not die a martyr's death; tradition also says it was this same John who was exiled to the island of Patmos under the

emperor Domitian, this same John who "was in the Spirit on the
Lord's day, and ... heard behind [him] a loud voice like a trumpet"
(Rev. 1:10 ESV).

He turned to see the Alpha and Omega, the First and the Last,
standing in the midst of seven lampstands, holding seven stars in his
right hand. His face, as John had seen once before on the Mount of
Transfiguration, shone like the sun.

John's book of Revelation, written after that vision, is a mas-
terpiece of apocalypse, of symbol and cryptic meaning. While the
overarching point of the book is the clearest thing in the world—God
wins, forever, over every enemy—the way that John's words carry
that point are veiled. Visions of the end weave through symbolic letters to seven churches in the world (themselves "seven lampstands"),
through visions of monsters birthed from the horrific black depths
of the sea, visions of trees, of darkening suns, of fire and blood and
judgment, and light beyond any thought of the sun's light on earth.
Visions of lambs and restorations. Of the perfection of the "seven
spirits of God" (the Spirit seen as seven lamps before the throne).
Visions of the seven stars in the right hand of Jesus, symbols of perfect
authority, clearly stated to be the messengers of the seven churches
to whom Christ wrote through John—symbols of perfection, of the
immanence of the Spirit through the body of Christ.

The prophet Zechariah, centuries before John, had a vision
too. "What do you see?" an angel asked the man of God. Zechariah
replied:

> "I see a lampstand all of gold, with a bowl on the
> top of it; there are seven lamps on it, with seven

> lips on each of the lamps that are on the top of
> it. And by it there are two olive trees, one on the
> right of the bowl and the other on its left." I said
> to the angel who talked with me, "What are these,
> my lord?" Then the angel who talked with me
> answered me, "Do you not know what these are?"
> I said, "No, my lord." He said to me, "This is the
> word of the LORD to Zerubbabel: Not by might,
> nor by power, but by my spirit, says the LORD of
> hosts." (Zech. 4:2–6)

The light at the end of the world, the light of might, the light of
John and Zechariah, of the seven churches, the seven stars—this is
the light of the Holy Spirit. Perfect in illumination, fueled in bright
burning by the oil of holiness, the Spirit sheds light on the end of
the world.

The Comforter soothes; soothes and invites.

The hope of re-creation lives in everything that has ever been
made or marred in our world so good and so bent. The hope of
re-creation lives in the life of seeds, in the dormant stump on the
borders of the wilderness mountain. It lives in the skin of the fingers, the stars set in the hands of craftsmen. The hope of re-creation
glitters in the butterflies, the moss agates waiting on the shores of
the river. It flashes in the bellies of catfish, in the hue of red apples,
in the barbed iron and cacti of the Golan Heights. The hope of re-
creation cries with the raven and the dove above the flood, bounds
like the deer with a star in its flank, roars with the lion that chases
to play or to prey, splashes with the pilgrims who dive into the

river, holds its breath like the boy hanging under the surface of the black lake.

Hope is everywhere; there is nowhere in creation that it does not cry out for the life of God that the Spirit promises.

THE HOPE OF RE-CREATION
LIVES IN EVERYTHING.

The hope is for the original very good, but it does not stop there. God is ever a doer of new things, and the re-creation will be good, even in its scars, in a depth and strength of goodness that the original creation was not capable of. Whatever loss and destruction and pain the brutality of all wrong things have wreaked on the world, the coming restoration will go limitlessly, effortlessly, joyously beyond—catching up the whole world in the arms of God and laughing for eternity, the doors to all things thrown open.

Hallelujah!

The descending sun, the true dawn of Christ come again, will consume the earth in a burning at once inexorable and good. The fire from above will devour, but how happy that devouring! In the end, whatever pain of burning, it will be a joy to be refined, the joy of compressing like carbon, turning into Hopkins's "immortal diamond."[1]

The nature of God is love, and all of everything must settle accounts with the fierce Lover, the Bridegroom of heaven, the ultimate Beloved. We will see in that flashing moment that existence has always been an invitation, can be nothing other than an invitation—an invitation and a joyful acceptance forever and ever.

All shall be well. All manner of things shall be well.

World without end.

There is nothing else to say.

I can only invite; rather, I can only repeat the invitation that has been passed to me, written in the words of John, written in the water of the riverbeds, in the skin of my fingers, in the high grass.

Come.

If you have ears, hear what the Spirit says to the churches, to the church. To you. To me.

Come.

The Spirit invites us to join his greater invitation, the one that is eternal but that never gets old. He calls you and me and all the rest of the bride to join him in calling Jesus, to come, to break like desolating light over every evil and darkness, to drive away the night, to bring eternal morning, to laugh over us joyously, like a strong man about to run a race.

Longing for Jesus with the ancient longing of the Trinity's love, the Spirit and the bride say, "Come." *We* say, "Come," in our very groaning for the re-creation. In that one word is invitation and pleading, expectation and confidence, hope, faith, love distilled.

"Come!"

The Spirit of creation calls Jesus to come, to re-create all things according to the Father's will.

The Spirit of inspiration calls Jesus to come, to lead all peoples to make and do and create and serve, all as if the light of the heavens illuminated our hands.

The Spirit of prophecy calls Jesus to come, to overturn every evil power, human or inhuman, every ruler or system that oppresses or tramples down his beloved ones.

The Spirit of both speaking and silence calls Jesus to come in his own way, to break mountains and to whisper, to cast down our expectations, to remind us of who is God and who is us.

The Spirit who empowered the promised Messiah calls him to come in the power that was promised to the good King from the beginning—to crush the serpent, to build a house for God, to establish an eternal, peaceable kingdom on earth as it is in heaven.

The Spirit who renews the earth calls Jesus to complete what has been well begun, to usher in a new age of life and sustaining, to let the glory of God cover the earth as the water covers the sea.

The Spirit who is poured out on all flesh calls Jesus to come with the happy expectation of apocalypse, of revelation, of the promised end that itself is a glorious beginning.

"Come!"

The stars fade.

The lamps are lit, and in the fading dark, the invitation rings louder still:

"*Come!*"

The Spirit, the descending Dove, calls Jesus to come, the first Beloved touching earth a second, perfect time, the victorious one, his hand on the locked door.

The Spirit, the wind of the wilderness, calls Jesus to raise up every valley and flatten every mountain, to cause the desert to explode in bloom, to flower with life, a lush garden in a land where only death used to whistle.

The Spirit, who brings the second birth from above, calls Jesus to end the labor pains of creation, birthing the universe anew as the church has been birthed, as everyone in Christ has been birthed into a nature eternal, limitlessly alive.

THE SPIRIT INVITES US TO JOIN HIS GREATER INVITATION, THE ONE THAT IS ETERNAL BUT THAT NEVER GETS OLD.

The Spirit of Pentecost, flaming out in pure speech, calls Jesus to come, to end the scattering, yet to scatter us anew, to gather us in, many and one. To let all the human family flourish in the unity of diversity.

The Spirit, the oil of holiness, calls Jesus the Anointed One to pour out the rich anointing of a new creation, holy and unassailable, over the heads of all his people, his stewards and siblings made according to his nature, formed in his likeness, to bear forever fruit after their kind.

The Spirit, the one breath and baptism of the one body, calls Jesus, the head of the body, to come, to forever make us one beyond any separation or schism, any wounding or division, to fulfill his prayer on the night he was betrayed that we all may be one as God himself is forever one.

The Spirit, the light forever, the seven lamps before the throne of the one who is radiant with uncreated light, calls simply, with and through and beyond our voices, calls from himself, calls to himself.

"COME!"

The lampstands blaze into flame eternal, the flame of all love and righteous judgment, the consuming fire, the fire of infinity, mathematical and everlasting, fire beyond any suns or imaginings of suns. They blaze! All things are illuminated, stark in clarity, shadowless.

"COME!"

I am not alone under the holy, waiting waters. Swimmers surround me, hoping, turning sunward. We divers below the black waters are illuminated, very light of very light bursting around our bodies like the rending of atoms, the great bubbles of my first scream lit like stars, hanging eternally above me, worlds of fire, orbiting solar systems—like globes of breath, huge gaps of hope and presence and life and love and wonder and *yes*!

The swimmers see!

They rise!

I see!

I rise!

"COME!"

I break through the surface of the water, surrounded by the first-fruits of a new creation, hands raised to heaven. Do you see what I am seeing? I feel sixteen again and sixty already and six hundred thousand years old in my journey around the sun. You and I and everything that the Spirit is calling up into life is being redeemed, united by grace through faith, with Christ the God-man. All is cold against the outside of my skin and burning like tongues of fire against the inside.

It is raining in great gray peels. These hands that slap against the black waves are deliciously temporal; they move like bird wings, a raven perhaps, or a dove. I am so far from alone, I was *never* alone—you are there, all God's children are there splashing joyously in the water too.

YOU AND I AND EVERYTHING THAT THE SPIRIT IS CALLING UP INTO LIFE IS BEING REDEEMED, UNITED BY GRACE THROUGH FAITH, WITH CHRIST THE GOD-MAN.

We are all a glorious symphony, a song for the endless ages chanted by the Spirit, that giver of life who ever calls out our names in harmony with the chorus of his teeming creation.

We do not need to open our eyes to see the stars; they burn behind everything with the ancient flame, the ferocity of the Spirit of all love and all danger, God himself, who dwells in unopposable light yet chooses, winking, to wander with us in this foreign maze, this darkness, for a spell. We all cry out above the waters now, a screaming, laughing shout of exultation, of abandon, of the very good, of the *yes!*

Oh! The fire is here, has always been here, speaking to you and to me and to the whole world the Spirit of God loves so dearly.

"It's good that you are; how wonderful that you exist!"

We can hear his voice around, throughout, shouting with us, joyful, thrice blessed, shouting through all that can be seen or splashed or tasted, the frigid water around our waists like the Jordan, the invisible bird in the tree, the sun that will descend tomorrow. We can see in a moment the God who loves us infinitely, the First and Last, who gives himself away to us. Our beginning and the end. This is our creation and re-creation, the eternal invitation of love. God has shown the door. We call. He calls. We open. He opens.

Even the face of the deep opens its mouth to praise him!

I shiver, but not from the cold.

Here we begin to know the Spirit.

I laugh. I weep. I splash. I call to you.

I turn myself and turn myself again.

I swim forever to the shore.

"AND THERE WAS NO MORE SEA."

Amen.

From the beginning, no one in the world has ever been truly alone. And now, at the moment you read this, the Spirit of God surrounds *you*.

His fire burns just outside your peripheral vision, illuminating your life. His care, his love, his truth, his peace, his justice—they are everywhere.

He longs for you to see him, to feel him. He longs to be known in the way that he has always known you. He desires you, beloved of God, his temple, his house. He loves *you*.

The Spirit is not far from any one of us, but he awaits your invitation.

Won't you ask him to perch nearer than before?

God bless you.

PERSONAL REFLECTIONS

THE ICONS

The images in this book are the result of a wonderful collaboration with well-known visual artist Martin French. Here are a few of our thoughts behind them.

SEVEN STARS

The Face of the Deep (page 23)

Paul: I love this image. We chose a raven for the symbol of creation in keeping with many creation and bringing-of-light tales of the indigenous Northwest tribes. I was thrilled to find a few obscure ancient Christian references to the Spirit at creation as a dark bird (before light was made). Even the star carries the good darkness here.

Martin: I find ravens endlessly fascinating. This serves as the perfect lead image for these icons.

Tooling the Creators (page 37)

Paul: Without knowing my arrowhead story, Martin placed the second star in the open palm of a hand. The line (watch for that in every image!) swirls, drawing us in, drawing inspiration out from the star.

Martin: The hand of the maker—a symbol loaded with possibilities. I left this image very simple, as a contrast to the rich spiritual ideas that swirl within it.

The Power of Prophets (page 51)

Paul: Watch the star descend into the prophet's mind, illuminating him and turning his head heavenward. By the way, everyone who sees this asks if it is my profile (has my nose). It's wicked Saul's, so I hope not. It's not … Right, Martin? Martin?

Martin: Perhaps a subconscious portrait. We shall never know.

The Voice of the Mountain (page 69)

Paul: Visually, this is one of my favorite images of the collection. The ascent and descent, the light and dark, the star like a sunrise; it's all here in hulking power.

Martin: One of my favorites as well. I wrestled with this one, trying to capture the mountain as a place of sacred encounter.

From the Stump of Jesse (page 87)

Paul: Martin initially felt that this was too thin and spindly as an image. "Perfect," I said. The frailty of the sprout under the star speaks to the frailty of the Messiah in Isaiah's metaphor.

Martin: Yes, challenging to say the least. My inclination would have been to create a very different "portrait" of Messiah. But this understated graphic speaks to the surprise of his life and ministry.

The Renewer of Earth (page 105)

Paul: Beautiful. Sustaining. Enough said.

Martin: I explored many different ideas for this one, searching for the right symbol. Once I got the running stag, it felt in rhythm with Paul's content.

Poured on All Flesh (page 125)

Paul: The whole cosmos, contained in a butterfly, symbol of metamorphosis, end and beginning, the "new thing."

Martin: The form of a butterfly is so nuanced, I was hesitant to present it in such a simplified form. My hope is that the symbolic depth and dynamic shapes will direct the reader into the rich ideas of this chapter.

SEVEN LAMPSTANDS

The Dove of the Beloved (page 143)

Paul: At least four symbols of the Spirit are at play here: dove, wind, fire, and light. Am I missing any?

Martin: These are the ideal set of raw materials for creating an icon.

The Wind of the Wilderness (page 161)

Paul: Love this. The lion is coming together (or coming apart), a "kindly predator," made of windy fire. I think the dove from the image before transformed into this beast to chase us into the desert.

Martin: The perfect visual prompt that became the most difficult image to "find" in the series. After many unsuccessful tries, a good friend reminded me of what I do best, and this is the result. I still want to illustrate this chapter with a set of ten large-scale posters of my different visual ideas here.

The Birth from Above (page 179)

Paul: My favorite image of the collection. The man on fire preparing for birth speaks for itself. But I am most intrigued by the hole in his ankle—a reference to our union with Jesus, like the apostle Paul says, in his life and death?

Martin: When Paul suggested this visual idea, I saw it in my mind immediately. It was a month or more before I actually drew it, but it came together effortlessly, as if I'd drawn it a hundred times. A moment of perfect creative collaboration.

The Flame of Pure Speech (page 199)

Paul: Visually, this reminds me of the icon for "Voice of the Mountain." The ziggurat, ancient Mesopotamian tower, is set on fire like a lamp. Babel turns into Pentecost.

Martin: I so didn't want to draw a ziggurat. But it works, doesn't it?

The Oil of Holiness (page 219)

Paul: Dramatic! I love the oil on the forehead, in the traditional mark of Christian anointing since the beginning. The person, saturated with holy oil, is aflame. We become the Spirit's lamp in our holiness, shedding his light.

Martin: The moody, intense portrait, in some ways very different than the other icons, creates a face-to-face encounter with the reader at an important point in the visual narrative.

The Breath of One Body (page 241)

Paul: Why does a chapter about breath have a stunted tree? It's the sprout, the body of Christ from the fifth star, all grown up. Grown up and sadly marred by disunity. The contours echo for me a system of veins, transit of oxygen, perhaps even the bronchial system leading to our lungs.

Martin: As with the icon of the sprout, the tree image is a challenging visual idea. They echo one another, creating a more complete story when considered together.

Come (page 261)

Paul: Pure invitation. Fire and stars, sperm and egg, the globe, a drop of water, the whirlpool of the face of the deep turning to re-creation by the Spirit. So powerful.

Martin: And it's an exclamation point to conclude the series. Bam!

ACKNOWLEDGMENTS

Enormous thanks are due to the many people who were part of bringing this book into the world:

To Andrew Stoddard, whose vision for this book exceeded even mine at the critical moment.

To Tim Peterson and the whole team at David C Cook for their care and craftsmanship.

To Martin French for giving so much of his time and brilliance to put pictures to a young man's words.

To professional friends and mentors in writing, particularly Marshall Shelley, Drew Dyck, Skye Jethani, Matt Woodley, and Marian Liautaud.

To Don and Blair Jacobson for their encouragement in my literary endeavors.

To the Franciscan Sisters of the Holy Eucharist in Bridal Veil, Oregon, for their neighborly joy and Christian hospitality.

To the monks of Mount Angel Abbey, particularly Father Pius, for welcoming me as a guest and for their tolerance as I pulled roughly 50 percent of their books out of their proper places.

To the Church of the Resurrection in Wheaton, Illinois, and Theophilus Church in Portland, Oregon, for the life of community.

To theological teachers and mentors, particularly Garry Friesen, Ray Lubeck, Domani Pothen, and Gerry Breshears.

To Father Stephen Gauthier for his spiritual direction and kindness, and pastors A.J. Swoboda and Cameron Marvin for their friendship and encouragement.

To the Oktober Klub (Kevin, Ashley, Laura) for their wild friendship.

To the Vaux Swifts writing group for "killing my darlings."

To the authors of every book I have ever read, worth it or not.

To everyone who has ever prayed on my behalf.

To all my friends across the world who have been Christ to me.

To all my family by blood, particularly Aunt Pam and Uncle Jim for pizza and conversation during the writing process, and to Steve and Debbie Downing for their help and hospitality in making our lives, let alone this book, possible during the whirlwind of 2014.

To my grandparents, now walking brighter trails, each of whom, in their own ways, saw beauty and truth in everything.

To my parents for sharing their love of the Bible and filling our house with books.

To Luke and Allison, friends who stick closer than a brother.

To my daughter, Elaia, and sons, Emmaus and Markos Arcturus, for teaching me joy and childlikeness, and for their voices in the apple tree (I love you three more than words can say).

And lastly but firstly, to my wife, Emily, without whose inexhaustible patience, encouragement, support, challenge, wisdom, and artistic vision, neither this work nor who I am today would be a reality. Darling, you will always be the beloved.

And truly lastly and firstly, to the Holy Spirit who proceeds from the Father and the Son, the Dove of heaven, the wind of the wilderness, the flame of Pentecost, the raven of creation, the great giver of all life, all beauty, all truth, and all wisdom—I am yours. Burn me alive.

To all of you,
       near and far,
             named and unnamed,
                   this book is given in abiding thanks.

P

NOTES

The Face of the Deep

1. "The Creation and the Emergence," from "Creation Stories from around the World: Encapsulations of Some Traditional Stories Explaining the Origin of the Earth, Its Life, and Its Peoples," 4th ed., University of Georgia, July 2000, www.gly.uga.edu/railsback/CS/CSCreation&Emergence.html.

2. Snorri Sturluson, *The Prose Edda: Tales from Norse Mythology,* trans. Jean I. Young (Los Angeles: University of California Press, 1966), 32.

3. "The Story of Corn and Medicine," from "Creation Stories," www.gly.uga.edu /railsback/CS/CSCorn&Medicine.html.

4. "The Naba Zid-Wendé," from "Creation Stories," www.gly.uga.edu/railsback /CS/CSNabazidWende.html.

5. "The Four Creations," from "Creation Stories," www.gly.uga.edu/railsback/CS /CSFourCreations.html.

6. "The Moon and the Morning Star," from "Creation Stories," www.gly.uga.edu /railsback/CS/CSMoon&Morningstar.html.

7. "Pan Gu and Nü Wa," from "Creation Stories," www.gly.uga.edu/railsback/CS /CSPG&NW.html.

8. Everett Fox, *The Schocken Bible,* vol. 1: *The Five Books of Moses* (New York: Schocken, 1995), 11–12.

9. Josef Pieper, *About Love* (Chicago: Franciscan Herald, 1974), 24.

Tooling the Creators

1. Mario Vargas Llosa, *Letters to a Young Novelist,* trans. Natasha Wimmer (New York: Picador, 2003), 7.

2. John Ruskin, *On Art and Life: You Must Either Make a Tool of the Creature, or a Man of Him. You Cannot Make Both* (New York: Penguin, 2005), 5, 12, 14, 20, 25.

3. Peter Washington, ed., *Hopkins: Poems by Gerard Manley Hopkins,* "As Kingfishers Catch Fire" (New York: Alfred A. Knopf, 1995), 18.

The Power of Prophets

1. "American Fact Finder: Antelope City, Oregon," United States Census Bureau, http://factfinder.census.gov/faces/nav/jsf/pages/community_facts.xhtml.

2. "Rajneesh," *Wikipedia,* https://en.wikipedia.org/wiki/Rajneesh.

3. Stephen King, *The Stand* (New York: Anchor, 2012), 918.

The Voice of the Mountain

1. Jerome T. Walsh, *Berit Olam: Studies in Hebrew Narrative and Poetry, I Kings,* ed. David W. Cotter (Collegeville, MN: Liturgical, 1996), 275.

2. Walsh, *Berit Olam,* 266.

3. Paul Hawken, "Commencement: Healing or Stealing?," University of Portland, www.up.edu/commencement/default.aspx?cid=9456.

4. "Shane Clairborne Quotes," Goodreads, http://www.goodreads.com /quotes/1281343-it-s-hard-to-hear-the-gentle-whisper-of-the-spirit.

5. Dr. Robert Stackpole, "The Fate of 'Talkative Souls,' the Value of Silence: Dr. Robert Stackpole Answers Your Questions on Divine Mercy," *The Divine Mercy,* April 4, 2007, www.thedivinemercy.org/library/article.php?NID =2619Blog.

From the Stump of Jesse

1. C. S. Lewis, *Mere Christianity* (New York: HarperCollins, 2015), 50.

2. Walter Brueggemann, *Isaiah 1–39* (Louisville, KY: John Knox, 1998), 99.

3. Brueggemann, *Isaiah 1–39,* 99.

4. David Rosenberg, *A Literary Bible* (Berkeley, CA: Counterpoint, 2009), 222.

The Renewer of Earth

1. Abraham Kuyper, *The Work of the Holy Spirit,* trans. Henri DeVries (New York: Funk and Wagnalls, 1900), 47.

2. Basil the Great, quoted in George Anson Jackson, *The Post-Nicene Greek Fathers* (New York: Appleton and Company, 1883), 98–99.

3. Lord Alfred Tennyson, "In Memoriam," The Literature Network, www.online-literature.com/tennyson/718/.

4. Dumitru Stăniloae, *The Experience of God: Orthodox Dogmatic Theology,* vol. 2, *The World: Creation and Deification,* trans. and ed. Ioan Ionita and Robert Barringer (Brookline, MA: Holy Cross Orthodox Press, 2000), 172.

5. Annie Dillard, *Pilgrim at Tinker Creek* (New York: HarperCollins, 1998), 146–47.

6. Walter Cradock, quoted in Congregational Historical Society, *Transactions,* vol. 12–13 (London: Congregational Historical Society, 1969), 20.

7. Alexander Schmemann, *O Death, Where Is Thy Sting?* (New York: St Vladimir's Seminary, 2003), 86.

8. Schmemann, *O Death,* 86.

9. Tennyson, "In Memoriam."

10. Tennyson, "In Memoriam."

11. A. W. Tozer, *The Knowledge of the Holy* (New York: HarperCollins, 2009), 75.

12. Basil the Great, quoted in David Anderson, *St Basil the Great: On the Holy Spirit* (New York: St. Vladimir's Seminary, 1980), 23–24.

13. The author found this prayer in an out-of-print prayer book translation in the basement library at the Mount Angel Abbey and Seminary in Oregon.

14. Walter Cradock, quoted in Geoffrey F. Nuttall, *The Holy Spirit in Puritan Faith and Experience* (Chicago: University of Chicago Press, 1992), 137.

Poured on All Flesh

1. Gerard Manley Hopkins, "Pied Beauty," Bartleby.com, www.bartleby.com/122/13.html.

The Dove of the Beloved

1. Henry Wadsworth Longfellow, "My Lost Youth," www.bartleby.com/102/69 .html.

2. C. S. Lewis, *The Four Loves: An Exploration of the Nature of Love* (New York: Mariner, 1971).

3. "Pablo Picasso Quotes," ThinkExist, http://thinkexist.com/quotation/each _second_we_live_is_a_new_and_unique_moment_of/339726.html.

4. Thomas Merton, *I Have Seen What I Was Looking For,* ed. M. Basil Pennington (New York: New City, 2005), 229.

5. Henri Nouwen, *Life of the Beloved* (New York: Crossroad, 2002), 113.

6. Peter Washington, ed., *Hopkins: Poems by Gerard Manley Hopkins,* "As Kingfishers Catch Fire" (New York: Alfred A. Knopf, 1995), 18.

The Wind of the Wilderness

1. Alan Paton, *Cry, the Beloved Country* (New York: Scribner, 2003), 116.

2. Madeleine L'Engle, *Walking on Water* (New York: North Point, 1995), 13.

The Birth from Above

1. C. S. Lewis, *The Screwtape Letters* (New York: HarperCollins, 2001), 37.

2. Hermes Mercurius Trismegistus, *The Emerald Tablet of Hermes* (New York: Merchant, 2013).

The Flame of Pure Speech

1. Saint Macarius, quoted in A. J. Mason, *Fifty Spiritual Homilies of St. Macarius the Egyptian* (New York: Macmillan, 1921), 183–84.

2. "Antoine de Saint-Exupéry Quotes," Goodreads, www.goodreads.com /quotes/384067-if-you-want-to-build-a-ship-don-t-drum-up.

The Oil of Holiness

1. Morgan Llwyd, quoted in Geoffrey F. Nuttall, *The Holy Spirit in Puritan Faith and Experience* (Chicago: University of Chicago Press, 1992), 140.

2. John of the Cross, quoted in Kieran Kavanaugh, ed., *John of the Cross: Selected Writings* (New Jersey: Paulist, 1987), 169.

3. Augustine, "Prayers," Catholic Online, www.catholic.org/prayers/prayer.php ?p=81.

The Breath of One Body

1. Father Stephen Freeman, "Baptism and the Final Destruction of Demons," *Glory to God for All Things,* January 6, 2014, http://blogs.ancientfaith.com /glory2godforallthings/2014/01/06/baptism-and-the-final-destruction-of -demons/.

Come

1. Gerard Manley Hopkins, "That Nature Is a Heraclitean Fire and of the Comfort of the Resurrection," Bartleby.com, www.bartleby.com/122/48.html.

CONTACT THE AUTHOR

If you enjoyed this book, Paul would love to hear from you.
You can write him at:

Paul J. Pastor
PO Box 36
Bridal Veil, OR 97010

Continue the conversation and get updated on Paul's latest projects
by visiting www.pauljpastor.com.

At David C Cook, we equip the local church around the corner and around the globe to make disciples. Come see how we are working together—go to **www.davidccook.org**. Thank you!